Men-at-Arms • 127

The Israeli Army in the Middle East Wars 1948–73

John Laffin • Illustrated by Mike Chappell

Series editor Martin Windrow

First published in Great Britain in 1982 by Osprey Publishing,
Midland House, West Way, Botley, Oxford OX2 0PH, UK
44-02 23rd St, Suite 219, Long Island City, NY 11101, USA
Email: info@ospreypublishing.com

Osprey Publishing is part of the Osprey Group.

Transferred to digital print on demand 2009

First published 1982
13th impression 2004

Printed and bound in Great Britain

A CIP catalogue record for this book is available from the British Library

ISBN: 978 0 85045 450 5

Filmset in Great Britain

Publisher's note
The colour plates in this book are the fruits of research carried out jointly by the author, editor and artist. Osprey are grateful to
G Cornish for his assistance.
   The difficulties of publishing hard information about the Middle East Wars are well known; many Arabs consider themselves to still
be at war, and the requirements of both security and propaganda present major obstacles to the objective writer. This former applies
particularly to the identification of specific units and their insignia. While Osprey are confident that this book represents a considerable
advance over previously published material, it is inevitable that some areas are still obscure. The tables of units involved in the various
campaigns, compiled from a number of Israeli and Arab sources, cannot be cross-checked to the degree we would wish; and in some
cases identification by commander's name only has ben unavoidable. Interested readers will find the titles listed on p. 39 of value.
The major work by Brigadeer El-Edroos is particularly relevant; although a 'commissioned' history, and therefore to be approached
with care, it covers a far wider area than its title might suggest, and in great depth. The editor has leant heavily on Brig. El-Edroos's
table of unit deployment.

The Woodland Trust
Osprey Publishing is supporting the Woodland Trust, the UK's leading woodland conservation charity, by funding the
dedication of trees.

www.ospreypublishing.com

The Israeli Army in the Middle East Wars 1948-73

The Israeli Approach

Unlike other nations, Israel does not face an enemy whose sole aim is to defeat its army or to conquer a specified area of land. Various Arab leaders have called for the total destruction of the Jewish state, and Israel regards Middle East conflict as nothing less than a war for Israel's existence. Many nations have lost wars and yet continued to exist in one way or another—Israel assumes in advance that defeat in war means an end to the Jewish nation, and it wages war accordingly. This factor must be grasped to understand Israel's approach to its army and to the strategy, tactics, training and conduct of war.

The Israeli philosophy of defence is fourfold: firstly, the war must not be fought in Israel, so as to avoid civilian casualties and damage. Secondly, Israel must seize and retain the initiative. The

Israelis have only once been pre-empted—in the Yom Kippur or October War of 1973. Thirdly, wars must be short—Israel cannot afford to fight a long war, as even long periods of mobilisation disrupt the nation's fragile economy. Fourthly, heavy casualties must be avoided. This last might seem obvious; but in Israel, with its close-knit family ties, its strictly limited manpower and its special economic considerations, casualties assume a unique political importance.

The General Staff cannot think in terms of a 'final decision' over the Arabs, but only of defeating them in particular battles and wars. It aims to inflict heavy losses on the enemy to deter any renewed attacks.

Surrounded by hostile nations, the tiny state has depended since 1948 on the efficiency of its armed services. They have fought six victorious wars,

Dramatic study of an Israeli mechanised column headed by a Sherman tank moving through the desert dawn to attack Egyptian positions in the Sinai. (Author's collection)

Typical Zahal tank crewman of the 1960s, wearing the old American crash helmet with added radio equipment. The high peak of efficiency achieved by the Armoured Corps under Maj.Gen. Tal's leadership enabled such crews to defeat much larger enemy forces with newer equipment. Gunnery skills, and the technical know-how to keep tanks running in combat conditions, combined with tactical expertise to produce extraordinary results.

perhaps for medical reasons, are profoundly dejected and often suffer from a feeling of shame. The vast majority of young men and most young women want the experience of serving in the forces, and would be volunteers if this were legally possible. There is no such thing as voluntary enlistment; nobody can voluntarily join the regular army at any age unless he has served as a conscript or draftee. In this Israel may be unique.

Most young Israelis believe that not to serve in the forces excludes them from a vital experience. Israel has become a garrison state in which Army and society are inseparable because of the endless fight for survival.

Yigal Yadin, who organised the Army after its first war, said that every male citizen of Israel is a soldier on 11 months' leave. It is a pointed way of describing a new-model citizen army, which could be copied with advantage by many smaller nations finding it difficult to balance their economy and yet spend large sums on defence.

Israel's Army is divided into two major components. First are the regulars (Sherut Qevah), made up of the career soldiers and those doing their three-year service. Second are the reservists (Sherut Muim). Together they form Zahal-Zva Ha-Hagana Le-Yisrael — the Israel Defence Forces — or commonly just 'Zahal'.

though Israel's population—3.2 million at the time of the 1973 war—is only a fraction of the 53 million Arabs in the countries on Israel's borders. For these victories the Army—with expert air support—is largely responsible. For a force which began as an irregular, impoverished and improvised army it has a formidable record.

A major factor in Israeli military success is that while in most societies the Army is separate from society, in Israel no division exists, if only because the army is a citizen army. The regular professional element is very small, and the rest are conscripts. In many countries the word 'conscripts' has implications of unwilling men and women compelled to fight. This does not apply to Israel. An established tradition of service and an acceptance of military obligations as part of citizenship takes people into the forces both as a duty and as a privilege. Men who are rejected,

Israel's Six Wars

Israel's outlook on war is based on the need to survive, but the Army's proficiency is the result of practice. Its list of wars and operations, in the 25-year period 1947–1973 is probably unequalled in history:

First War 1947–1949 War of Independence or War of Liberation:

Civil War or Communal War phase: December 1947 to 14 May 1948. Many attacks by Arab irregulars and by Arab Liberation Army. Israelis fight 'the Battle of the Roads'.

Operation 'Nachshon' 2–20 April 1947. First Jewish attempt at a large-scale offensive to break through to Jerusalem.

Operation 'Yiftach' 7 May. Israeli conquest of Safed.

Fall of the Etzion Bloc Many Jews killed by Jordanians, who capture a group of kubbutzim.

Invasion phase:

Arab nations' invasion 15 May–10 June. Armies of Egypt, Syria, Lebanon, Iraq and Jordan invade.

First truce 11 June–9 July.

Counter-attack phase: The Ten Days' Offensive, 9–18 July.

Operation 'Dani' Jerusalem–Tel Aviv sector.

Operation 'Barosh' Syrian front.

Operation 'Dekel' Galilee sector.

Second truce 18 July–10 October.

Final phase begins: 10 October 1948.

Operation 'Yoav' 15–22 October, Negev and Sinai sectors.

Operation 'Ten Plagues' 15 October–8 November, Sinai, Negev, Hebron.

Operation 'Hiram' 28–31 October, Galilee–Lebanon front.

Operation 'Lot' 24–25 November, route opened to Dead Sea at Sodom.

Operation 'Horev' 22 December–7 January 1949, Gaza and Negev sectors. Rout of Egyptian Army.

Operation 'Uvdah' 6–10 March. Achievement of control of southern Negev and Judean deserts. Armistices were signed by the various Arab nations between 24 February and 20 July.

Second War, known as Sinai Campaign or Operation 'Kadesh'; 29 October–6 November 1956:

Outflanking of Egyptian line, 29 October.

Canal Zone and Mitla Pass operations, 30 October–1 November.

The workhorse of the mechanised forces since the War of Independence has been the Second World War vintage M3/M9 half-track series. These photos of mechanised infantry during the Six-Day War of 1967 show typical features of Zahal half-tracks: very heavy external stowage, and a locally-installed .30cal. MG position beside the driver.

Gaza Strip and Sharm el Sheikh operations, 25 November.

Third War, known as the Six–Day War, 5–10 June 1967:

Pre-war phase 1: 14 May, Egyptian advance into Sinai.

Pre-war phase 2: 16 May, UN forces withdraw from Sinai; Arabs mobilise for attack.

Pre-war phase 3: 22 May, Egypt closes Tiran Straits to Israeli shipping.

Operation 'Devastation' 5 June, Israel destroys Egyptian Air Force. By 10 June Israel beats the Egyptian, Syrian and Jordanian Armies, captures Sinai, West Bank, Golan Heights.

Fourth War, War of Attrition, sometimes known as the Electronics War, March 1969–7 August 1970. Almost incessant warfare along the Suez Canal, largely saturation shelling from the Egyptian side and retaliatory raids by the Israelis. This was the longest Israeli war, apart from the intermittent terrorist offensive.

Fifth War, Yom Kippur War, the October War or War of Atonement, 6–25 October 1973:

Golan Front: 6–10 October, Syrian offensive. 11–24 October, Israeli counter-offensive.

Suez Front: 6 October, Egyptian offensive; 7–9 October, Israeli counter-attack; 9–15 October, Israeli holding phase; 15–19 October, Operation 'Gazelle'—Israeli counter-invasion.

Sixth War, The Terrorist War: this has been continual, with peaks of infiltration and attacks by ambush and bomb, especially in 1955–6; 1964–9 and 1978–81.

The Mandate Period

During the earlier part of the British Mandate in Palestine—which lasted from the end of the First World War until mid-1948—defence of the Jewish settlements against the unending Arab attacks was officially in the hands of the Hashomer (Watchman) organisation. The British would permit no official Jewish force, so Hagana, an underground army, came into existence.

Behind Jewish military development was the teaching of Captain Orde Wingate, of the occupying British Army, who created a Jewish force with the title of 'Special Night Squads'. The purpose of these squads was to raid deep into enemy territory, undermining Arab morale and

Maj.Gen. Israel Tal, photographed beside one of the T-54/55s of the Egyptian Army knocked out by his armoured Ugda in northern Sinai in June 1967. As commander of the Armoured Corps 1964–69 Tal was an important innovator. His methods were highly successful in 1967, but were invalidated in 1973 under the new conditions created by the enemy's lavish use of hand-launched rockets and wire-guided missiles by strong infantry 'tank-hunter' teams. (Author's collection)

initiative and creating havoc. This approach is still clear in Israeli military policy. The Special Night Squads were the training-ground for many of the Army's later leaders, including Moshe Dayan; these men took with them from their Squad days the tactics of swift, decisive, surprise attacks. Hagana training stressed individual initiative and irregular military activities.

The activities of the Palmach—Hagana's 'regular' arm—demanded a high level of dedication and fitness. Among the 1,200 Palmachi soldiers who fell during the organisation's eight years of existence were 19 women, the most famous being Bracha Fuld, who died in 1946 in the defence of Tel Aviv.

A Jewish Brigade of the British Army fought with distinction during the Second World War and gained much valuable experience; many of these men arrived in Palestine after 1945. In addition, a number of individual Jews with military skills learned in the British and other armed forces came to Palestine between 1945 and 1948. These were the backbone of Hagana, which, in April–May 1948, was 29,677 strong, including 3,100 in the Palmach, the élite arm led by Yigal Allon.

The front-line troops were supported by the Field Army, the Home Guard and the Youth Battalions. The Field Army was similar to the British Territorials and amounted to no more than 10,000; the Home Guard consisted of all other adults who could use arms; the Youth Battalions were for boys of about 17, and were roughly comparable to British cadets.

Towards the end of 1947 Arabs raided more boldly and frequently, and Hagana came out into the open. David Ben Gurion assumed strategic control, though Israel Galil, the operations commander, had tactical control. In December, in anticipation of more trouble to come when the British pulled out, Hagana was organised into six geographical commands, and mobilisation and training were stepped up.

Unable to control the roads linking the isolated Jewish settlements, Hagana organised convoys. As they had no armour they produced many examples of the famous 'sandwich' home-made armoured car. This was a commercial vehicle covered by two layers of steel plates with concrete

poured between them. The 'Battle of the Roads', as it is known to the Israelis, lasted through the winter of 1947 until late spring 1948, and cost more than 1,000 Israeli lives.

In April 1948, with the British Mandate in its final stage, the Jews went over to the attack in Operation 'Nachshon'. The objective was to clear the road to besieged Jerusalem. Strategic points along the winding mountain road were captured and convoys passed unscathed for the first time. One action during this operation gave the fledgling Israeli Army one of its major traditions. A company of the Palmach's 'Harel' Brigade was forced to withdraw from the hilltop village of Kastel near Jerusalem. Because the Arabs were about to reach the hilltop the only way of saving at least part of the company was to leave a rearguard to hold the summit while the others retreated down the hillside. Knowing that the rearguard would almost certainly be cut off and killed, the company commander gave an order which has since been quoted in every Israeli officers' course: 'All privates will retreat, all commanders will cover their withdrawal.' The company commander himself stayed, and was killed together with the three platoon commanders and all but one of the section leaders.

War of Independence 1948-49

All-out war began the moment Israel became a state—approved as such by the United Nations—on 14 May 1948. The next day the armies of Egypt, Syria, Jordan, Iraq and Lebanon attacked. By military logic and weight of numbers they should have won the so-called 'Four Weeks War'. The Arabs had the geographic advantage because Jewish settlements were scattered in the coastal plains, in the northern Negev desert and in Galilee. Militarily speaking they were simply outposts surrounded by Arab territory, and the problems of communication and mutual support were immense.

The Arabs also had many more weapons of a higher standard than the Israelis. Hagana had about 10,000 rifles, some revolvers and Sten guns, 400 light machine guns, 180 medium machine guns, 670 2in. mortars and 93 3in. mortars. The new Army had only two field guns, of 65mm calibre, and little ammunition for them. Kibbutz

7

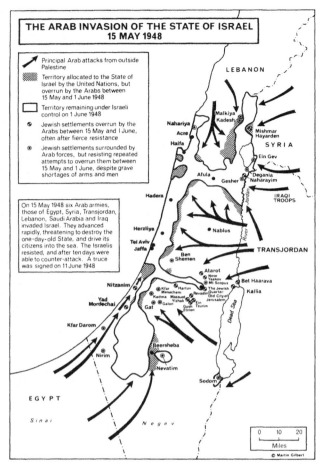

THE ARAB INVASION OF THE STATE OF ISRAEL 15 MAY 1948

↗ Principal Arab attacks from outside Palestine

▨ Territory allocated to the State of Israel by the United Nations, but overrun by the Arabs between 15 May and 1 June 1948

☐ Territory remaining under Israeli control on 1 June 1948

⊙ Jewish settlements overrun by the Arabs between 15 May and 1 June, often after fierce resistance

⊙ Jewish settlements surrounded by Arab forces, but resisting repeated attempts to overrun them between 15 May and 1 June, despite grave shortages of arms and men

On 15 May 1948 six Arab armies, those of Egypt, Syria, Transjordan, Lebanon, Saudi Arabia and Iraq invaded Israel. They advanced rapidly, threatening to destroy the one-day-old State, and drive its citizens into the sea. The Israelis resisted, and after ten days were able to counter-attack. A truce was signed on 11 June 1948

LEBANON
SYRIA
TRANSJORDAN
EGYPT
Sinai
Negev
IRAQI TROOPS

Malkiya Kadesh, Naharia, Acre, Haifa, Mishmar Hayarden, Ein Gev, Afula, Gesher, Degania, Naharayim, Hadera, Herzliya, Nablus, Tel Aviv, Jaffa, Ben Shemen, Atarot, Neve Yaakov, Mt Scopus, Bet Haarava, Nitzanim, Kfar Menachem, Hartuv, The Jewish Quarter Old City of Jerusalem, Revadim, Kallia, Yad Mordechai, Kedma, Massuot, Yizhak, Galon, Ein Tzurim, Gush Etzion, Gat, Kfar Darom, Beersheba, Nirim, Nevatim, Sodom

0   10   20
Miles
© Martin Gilbert

industrial initiative produced grenades, bombs and the 'Little David' mortar. Mines were small wooden crates filled with about 8kg of explosive and fitted with a primitive detonator mechanism.

Armour was non-existent until two British sergeants, sympathetic to the Jewish cause, stole two Cromwell tanks from the 3rd Hussars Depot near Haifa. Smashing through the unguarded gates, they kept a rendezvous with Hagana men and delivered the tanks to Tel Aviv. This was the foundation of the Israeli armoured corps. The next three tanks were Shermans rebuilt from scrap-heap material found in British ordnance depots around the country. During the war ten French Hotchkiss light tanks and some armoured cars and half-tracks were added to the 'corps'.

The Czech government was the only one to supply arms to Israel—the German Mauser Kar 98k rifle, ZB-37 heavy machine guns, and a locally produced variant of the wartime Messerschmitt Bf 109 fighter aircraft. From various sources—including hijacked European arms consignments to their Arab enemies—Hagana obtained the Sten and MP40 sub-machine guns and the Bren, 7.92mm Besa, German 7.92mm MG34, and US .30cal. and .50cal. Browning machine guns.

The Arab armies had an overwhelming preponderance in artillery, tanks and aircraft, but the Israelis had one great advantage—centralised command. The Arab armies had no overall high command; but among their disparate forces they did have the best army in the Middle East, the British-armed and trained Arab Legion from Jordan, which captured the Jewish quarter of the Old City of Jerusalem on 20 May.

With few reserves, the Israeli high command had to work on priorities. Jerusalem was seen as the main sector, and to prevent its complete isolation after the Jordanian coup the Arab towns of Lod and Ramallah were captured in a well-planned five-brigade action led by the Palmach commander, Yigal Allon. The 8th Armoured Bde. was the most interesting formation. Commanded by the veteran Yitzhak Sadeh, it consisted of a mixture of overseas immigrant groups, Hagana men, and even ex-British tank crew deserters. Of its two battalions the 82nd Tank Bn. was made up of an 'English' and a 'Russian' company—referring to the main languages spoken in units composed of former Western and Soviet army veterans. The 89th Mechanised Bn., a jeep-mounted commando unit, was led by the young Moshe Dayan.

One of the most important points along the Tel Aviv–Jerusalem Road was Latrun, where the Arab Legion held the old British police fortress. The Israelis made five separate attempts to capture the position, but all failed. In one attack 400 new immigrant soldiers serving in the 7th Brigade were killed, without ever knowing their country. In all, more than 700 men died before Latrun.

On 31 May the IDF—'Zahal'—was declared to be the one official army of Israel, thus outlawing the small terrorist groups such as Irgun Zvai Leumi (National Military Organisation) and the 'Stern Gang'. Even the Palmach was dissolved, because it was believed to be too 'political'. The first Chief-of-Staff was Yaacov Dori, but as he was

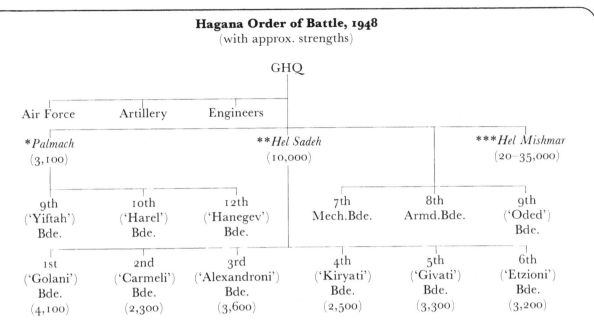

Hagana Order of Battle, 1948
(with approx. strengths)

GHQ

Air Force	Artillery	Engineers			

*Palmach (3,100)			**Hel Sadeh (10,000)		***Hel Mishmar (20–35,000)
9th ('Yiftah') Bde.	10th ('Harel') Bde.	12th ('Hanegev') Bde.	7th Mech.Bde.	8th Armd.Bde.	9th ('Oded') Bde.
1st ('Golani') Bde. (4,100)	2nd ('Carmeli') Bde. (2,300)	3rd ('Alexandroni') Bde. (3,600)	4th ('Kiryati') Bde. (2,500)	5th ('Givati') Bde. (3,300)	6th ('Etzioni') Bde. (3,200)

*'Palmach', 'Plugot Machatz' = 'Striking Companies'—full-time regular element of Hagana, formed 1941.
**'Hel Sadeh' = 'Mobile Field Corps'—part-time volunteers, mainly under Palmach leadership.
***'Hel Mishmar' = static home guard units; potentially, every able-bodied adult.
NB: The two underground organisations, Irgun and LEHI ('Stern Gang'), did not acknowledge Hagana leadership or control and operated in only the loosest co-operation with Hagana forces.

too ill the burden of command fell on Yigal Yadin, Chief of Operations. Yadin had been only 26 when he first held this post in Hagana, and even now he was only 30. Such youthfulness in high command was to become a feature of Zahal.

Israeli military successes in 1948 and in later years may owe much to the fact that the Jews lacked military traditions; this allowed unlimited scope for new ideas and original methods. One military attitude was set by Yigal Allon, who experienced some of the most desperate fighting of the war while in charge of Operation 'Yiftah' in Upper Galilee, 6–10 May. Safed, the key objective, was captured on 10 May after a series of daring attacks against Arab forces entrenched on commanding heights. The strategic aspect of the operation involved extreme risk-taking. While Allon was concentrating his forces around Safed the Jewish villages and kibbutzim were under fire from Lebanese and irregular forces with vastly superior firepower. Allon was responsible for the security of the area as a whole, but he chose to leave the settlements to fend for themselves so that

he could retain the initiative and launch the offensive on Safed. All the villages withstood the attacks; Safed fell to Allon, and the Arabs were forced to scatter their forces. Allon's strategy in that operation became Israeli doctrine.

A famous episode of the 'Dani' operation established a tradition for boldness. When Zahal attacked Lod the tanks of the 8th Bde. were supposed to provide close fire support to breach the fortifications of the perimeter. When the tanks failed to arrive the commander of the 89th Mech. Bn., Moshe Dayan, though lacking armour support, took his column forward behind an Arab Legion armoured car captured the previous day. Dayan's jeep-mounted troops broke through the fortified perimeter, drove across town at top speed, came out at the other side, and pressed on to the next objective. This breakthrough broke the defenders' morale, and Lod and Ramle were captured.

In the Negev, commandos from the south and Hagana from the north now simultaneously attacked the Egyptians. The result was the

A soldier of 'Motta' Gur's 55th Parachute Bde. during the Jerusalem street fighting of 6–7 June 1967. Note British-style paratroop helmet, French camouflage trousers, and Israeli armament and webbing. The famous 9mm Uzi sub-machine gun, seen here in its folding-butt version, has only nine principal parts. Cyclic rate of fire is 650rpm. (Author's collection)

capture of the key town of Beersheba and the encirclement of the 4th Egyptian Bde. at Faluja. The Egyptians were still strong, but with the Israelis in their rear they could no longer threaten Tel Aviv.

A week later the Israelis struck the Arab Liberation Army in northern Galilee, forcing it to retreat. One of the last offensives, 'Operation 'Horev', was also the largest. In a campaign that would have done credit to any German Panzer division the Israelis sent mobile columns of armed jeeps into the wastes of the Sinai; moving fast, they reached the airfields from which the Egyptians were raiding Israel. Only political intervention stopped the Israelis from wiping out the Egyptian Army—all it held by the end of Operation 'Horev' was the Gaza Strip.

The final and most spectacular operation was the race for Akaba. On 10 March 1949 two brigades seized the shores of the Gulf of Akaba and established a base—later, Eilat. Armistice negotiations on 20 May brought the war to an end.

The battles of the War of Independence were unit actions in which small formations attempted to gain local tactical advantage. Success depended almost entirely on personal leadership. For the Israelis this had been decisive, but they had lost 8,000 men and women in battle—a heavy price for the new nation of 600,000 and its army of 60,000. The losses had an important bearing on Zahal's planning and strategy. The major result was the decision that to make up for deficiency in numbers, Israel in future had to pre-empt Arab offensives.

Yadin became Chief-of-Staff, and made his main task the creation of a reserve army. He chose the Swiss system, in which every able-bodied man becomes a potential defender. Israeli reservists would belong to specific combat units, and on mobilisation would join their operational unit. The system would work if the reservists could actually perform as first-line combat troops.

In October 1948 the home-made ribbons and armbands worn by officers had been replaced by standard insignia based on a table of ranks. The Chief-of-Staff alone carried the highest rank, Rav-Aluf (a Biblical title), then equivalent to brigadier; other ancient titles were revived for the ranks of Aluf-Mishne (colonel), Sgan-Aluf (lieutenant-

Israeli soldiers at the Western Wall in the Old City of Jerusalem, soon after capturing it from Jordanian troops on 7 June 1967; their emotion at regaining this holiest of Jewish holy places is evident. (Author's collection)

colonel), Rav-Seren (major), Seren (captain), Segen (first lieutenant) and Segen-Mishne (second lieutenant). Though regulation pips, ribbons and uniforms were prescribed, the majority of Israeli soldiers continued to wear whatever clothes they liked—or could get—because there were not enough issue uniforms. With the coming of peace Zahal could concentrate on becoming an army.

Towards the '100 Hours War'

David Ben Gurion, founder of the Israeli Defence Forces, and Israel's first Defence Minister, had dreamed of making the IDF a farmer's army. He saw the IDF as a working army which would combine superior combat ability with an agricultural education to form a brotherhood of pioneer/fighters. To some extent Zahal did evolve according to Ben Gurion's dream, but Israeli society was already more complex, and not all Israelis were farmers. Also, a pioneer-soldier of the early 1950s needed greater military skills than Ben Gurion had envisaged. But the principle of youth at senior rank was established—Mordechai Makleff was appointed Chief-of-Staff at the age of 33.

One of Zahal's major problems in those early days was officer training. The army had lost the best of its officers in the War of Independence; only a small percentage of those remaining had professional training of any sort, and fewer still had completed an officers' course in the British Army or in Hagana. In the early 1950s an immense effort was put into officer training. Gen. Haim Laskov was given charge of the operation, of which the aim was to train 27,000 officers in 18 months. Under Laskov's direction 30 military schools were established and uniform methods of instruction were instituted. One of Laskov's first actions was to teach many officers English so that they could read foreign military literature.

After the War of Independence armoured units were organised into a regular brigade—the 7th—and an armour training school.

By 1953 Israel was under great pressure from terrorists infiltrating from Jordan or the Gaza Strip. Punitive actions were not effective, and in August 1953 Chief-of-Staff Makleff set up a special hand-picked, highly-trained formation—Unit 101—to operate against Arab infiltrator bases, under the young Ariel ('Arik') Sharon,

later a general and currently Israeli Defence Minister. Men of the new unit were not supposed to look like Zahal men—the United States and Britain regarded Arab terrorist incursions as 'non-governmental', and tolerated them, but were angry when Israeli Army units carried out reprisals. So it was decided that men of the new special unit could not wear uniforms or insignia.

Sharon had the direct and forceful attitude necessary for the job. When he had been intelligence officer with Northern Command, Dayan, the GOC, asked him to consider the possibility of capturing two Jordanians to be used as bargaining counters for two Israeli prisoners in the hands of the Arab Legion. Sharon gave some offhand reply. Taking another officer with him, he then drove to Sheikh Hussein bridge on the Jordanian border, captured two Arab Legionnaires at pistol point, and took them back to Dayan. 'I only asked him if it was possible,' Dayan said later, 'and he returned with two Arab Legion soldiers as if he had gone out to pick fruit in the garden.'

Sharon travelled all over Israel looking for

To give close support to tank units Israeli Ordnance developed the combination of an M9 half-track mounting a 120mm Soltam mortar. Here the weapon seems to be mounted on an old Sherman chassis—probably a re-worked M7 Priest 105mm SP howitzer, of which numbers were in service in 1967. (Christopher F. Foss)

Israeli recce troops photographed on the Golan front in 1967; note wire-cutting bar welded to the front of the jeep, and shrouded recoilless rifle mounted in its rear. Two of the soldiers (foreground) seem to be wearing load-carrying waistcoats over their smocks, incorporating many small pouches. The use of numerous pouches on a web harness, rather than a large pack, seems to be Israeli policy. (Author's collection)

intelligent and adventurous men to make up his 40-man unit. During the few months of its existence Unit 101 made many small raids, which were increasingly successful as the men came to excel in silent infiltration, night·fighting and fieldcraft.

Dayan merged Unit 101 with the paratroop battalion, and Sharon was appointed commander of this new composite formation, known as Unit 202. He worked out a new tactical method to replace the old 'fire and movement' tactics learned from the British. Instead of relying on heavy covering fire Sharon trained his men to approach an enemy trench system, by night, without firing at all. They would walk slowly and in total silence until fired upon; then they ran forward, firing on the move. Breaking into small assault groups, the paratroopers would not take on the enemy in the fire trenches but would jump into the communication trenches, running and shooting all the way to

the centre and out again. The teams kept moving until all the defenders were killed or captured.

Dayan, together with Sharon, raised the Army to a new level of effectiveness, largely by a deliberate policy of creating crack units. Other units then aspired to the standards set by Sharon and the paratroops he commanded. One of his rules was that there would be no return from an action if it had not been fulfilled. Dayan spoke in even more forthright terms: 'A commander who returns from an action without having carried it out and whose men have sustained less than 50 per cent casualties will be dismissed.'

Under Dayan the Armoured Corps remained relatively primitive. Israeli armour on the eve of the 1956 War consisted of about 200 Shermans, nearly all acquired from France, and some 100 AMX-13s from the same source. These equipped the tank battalions of the regular 7th Armd.Bde. (including the veteran 82nd Tank Bn. of 1948 fame) and the reserve 27th and 37th Armd.Bdes. Their rôle was seen at this time as purely supportive—Dayan was an infantry-minded general. Each brigade had strong half-track and/or lorried infantry units; Israel had slowly acquired a total of some 600 half-tracks by 1956. Self-propelled artillery consisted of about 60 105mm howitzers on the AMX-13 chassis.

Dayan developed the rôle of the parachute unit, and by 1956 its mobilised strength was one brigade—202nd Parachute Bde. To spread the 'paratroop spirit' in the Army as a whole Dayan ordered that every officer, irrespective of branch of service, would undergo jump training—including himself.

The 1956 War

The Sinai Campaign of 1956 was the result of secret plans laid jointly by the British and French —determined to punish Nasser for his national-isation of the Suez Canal—and the Israelis, whose aim was to stop terrorist infiltration and, more importantly, to 'bleed' Egypt's recent and worry-ing arms build-up from Soviet aid. When Nasser proceeded to close the Straits of Tiran to Israeli shipping another pressing reason for action arose, since this route was Israel's outlet to the Red Sea and the oceans beyond.

Dayan's plan was to outmanoeuvre the enemy strongholds in northern Sinai by taking control of the major road junctions and key positions. He ordered the infantry to break through with half-tracks and other vehicles; tanks would be brought up on transporters to save track-miles, and after fighting in support of the infantry where necessary they would again allow the mobile infantry to take the lead.

A 'long-stop' force was also briefed. At 1659hrs on 29 October 1956, 16 Dakota transports (one of them piloted by a woman) dropped 395 Israeli paratroops at the strategic Mitla Pass, 40 miles east of Suez. Sharon led the rest of 202nd Para-chute Bde. forward by road to link up with the air-dropped group. Another task force took Kusseima. The Egyptians heavily engaged the Mitla force, but by the evening of 30 October the Israelis held the pass.

Col. Uri Ben-Ari took his 7th Armd.Bde. through the Israeli infantry at Kusseima and rapidly enveloped the key Egyptian position at Abu Ageila by striking through Deika Pass; his

brilliant move stopped the Egyptians from rein-forcing the Sinai army. Egyptian armour moved along two routes to attack the 7th Armd.Bde., but the counter-attack never arrived—the Israeli Air Force knocked out more than 100 vehicles.

On the night of 31 October–1 November Israel's Northern Force, including Col. Haim Bar-Lev's 27th Armd.Bde. and the 1st ('Golani') Inf.Bde., attacked the Gaza Strip and broke through the Egyptian defences. That day the Egyptian High Command ordered all troops to pull back to the Suez Canal, and in the subsequent rout the Egyptian Army was badly mauled. Be-cause of Dayan's creation of special scouting units the Israelis knew the Sinai better than the Egyptians, who had been there for many years.

The outstanding success of Operation 'Kadesh' was the classic armoured attack. Ben-Ari's tanks infiltrated to the rear of the Egyptian positions at Abu Ageila, and after hard fighting broke Egyptian defences which the infantry were failing

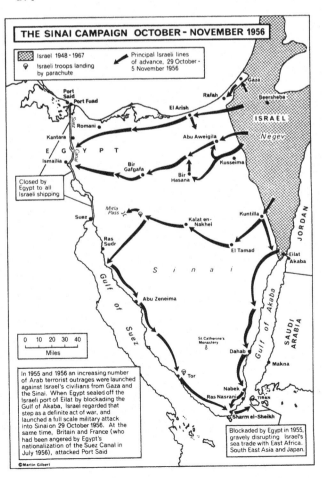

THE SINAI CAMPAIGN OCTOBER - NOVEMBER 1956

Israel 1948 - 1967
Israeli troops landing by parachute
Principal Israeli lines of advance, 29 October - 5 November 1956

Port Said
Port Fuad
Gaza
Rafah
Beersheba
El Arish
ISRAEL
Kantara
Romani
Abu Aweigila
Negev
EGYPT
Ismailia
Bir Gafgafa
Kusseima
Bir Hasana
Closed by Egypt to all Israeli shipping
Mitla Pass
Kalat en-Nakhel
Kuntilla
Suez
Ras Sudr
El Tamad
Eilat Akaba
JORDAN
Sinai
Abu Zeneima
Gulf of Suez
Gulf of Akaba
St. Catherine's Monastery
SAUDI ARABIA
Dahab
Makna
Tor
Nabek
Ras Nasrani
TIRAN
Sharm el-Sheikh

0 10 20 30 40
Miles

In 1955 and 1956 an increasing number of Arab terrorist outrages were launched against Israel's civilians from Gaza and the Sinai. When Egypt sealed off the Israeli port of Eilat by blockading the Gulf of Akaba, Israel regarded that step as a definite act of war, and launched a full scale military attack into Sinai on 29 October 1956. At the same time, Britain and France (who had been angered by Egypt's nationalization of the Suez Canal in July 1956), attacked Port Said

Blockaded by Egypt in 1955, gravely disrupting Israel's sea trade with East Africa, South East Asia and Japan.

©Martin Gilbert

Israeli Forces
October 1956 Campaign

202nd Airborne Bde. (Sharon)
of which one battalion (Eitan) air-dropped at Mitla Pass

Northern Task Force:
1st 'Golani' Inf.Bde.
12th Inf.Bde. (Elazar)
27th Mech.Bde. (Bar-Lev)—one mot.inf.bn., three sqns. Sherman, one sqn. AMX-13

Southern Task Force:
4th Inf.Bde.
10th Inf.Bde.
37th Mech.Bde.—two mot.inf.bns., one bn. Sherman, one sqn. AMX-13

Command Reserve:
7th Armd.Bde. (Ben-Ari)—82nd Tank Bn. (Sherman), 79th Tank Bn. (AMX-13), two mot.inf.bns.
9th Inf.Bde. (Yoffe)
Eilat—Sharm el Sheikh operation

to breach at the other end of the line. The 7th Armd.Bde. then rapidly moved west; the combat teams took control of most of central Sinai in a single day of non-stop advance. Even Dayan then had to admit that he had erred in his estimate of the tanks' capabilities.

Under their secret agreement with the Anglo-French forces the Israelis stopped their advance ten miles from the Canal; but this did not prevent them from capturing the Gaza Strip, and Sharm el Sheikh at the mouth of the Gulf of Akaba. They had taken the whole Sinai in just 100 hours.

In this lightning war the Israelis lost 151 dead and suffered 400 wounded. The Egyptians lost several thousand dead and wounded, and 6,000 were captured. Though UN action forced Israel to give up captured territory, the Israelis kept the considerable booty of military materiel which they had captured. They had acquired useful numbers of British, American and Soviet armoured vehicles capturing or destroying some 27 T-34/85s, 46 Shermans of various types, 60 APCs and about 60 SP guns, a good proportion of which were salvaged. They had also captured large quantities of small arms, ammunition, and towed artillery of calibres from 85mm up.

Dayan admitted that the armoured commanders had been right to chafe under the restrictions artificially placed upon them in pre-war manoeuvres and in the planning for Operation 'Kadesh'. Zahal now began its transition into an army built around large, mobile armoured formations; the Sinai Campaign thus served as an extensive exercise in preparation for the Six-Day War.

The Six-Day War

After the 1956 campaign Israel enjoyed a respite of 11 years before the next declared war, although terrorist infiltration continued, and the Syrians shelled the settlements of Galilee from the commanding Golan Heights at frequent intervals.

During this period Zahal grew considerably in size and effectiveness. Britain sold Israel some 250 Centurion Mk. III and V tanks; and the USA supplied some 200 M48 Pattons, at first secretly via the German Bundeswehr and later, from 1964, by direct shipment. Hawk anti-aircraft missiles were also supplied. Some 200 of the old Shermans were up-dated with a new French 105mm gun. About two battalions of reconditioned M7 Priest 105mm SP howitzers, and several batteries of 155mm weapons on Sherman chassis, were also added to the arsenal of the mobile forces. Further support for the tanks was provided by half-track 120mm mortar vehicles, half-track-mounted 90mm AT guns, and half-tracks with batteries of SS-11 wire-guided AT missiles. Among the infantry the standard personal weapon became the 7.62mm Belgian FN/FAL self-loading rifle, with the heavy-barrel version as the standard squad light automatic. Large numbers of the superb Israeli Uzi sub-machine gun were issued to paratroops, commandos, infantry junior leaders, and vehicle crews. The reliable US .30 and .50cal. Browning machine guns remained in widespread use.

After 1956 the tactical stress had been laid on mobility, and the armoured and mechanised brigades had been expanded at the expense of infantry. The typical armoured brigade fielded two battalions each of about 50 tanks; at least one half-track infantry battalion; brigade artillery, and a recce company. Armoured brigades were formed into divisional formations—Ugdas—with mechanised or lorried infantry brigades; the exact number of units within each Ugda, and their balance between armour and infantry, varied.

As Israeli Intelligence was well aware, however, the Arab arsenal was also becoming formidable, thanks to massive arms shipments from the Soviet bloc. Nevertheless it was not believed, in the spring of 1967, that war was imminent, if only because President Nasser of Egypt was still involved in an expensive and frustrating campaign in the Yemen. But the Russians were stirring up trouble by feeding Nasser false reports of Israeli intentions; and the Syrians, also anxious for a

Tank crewmen on the Suez front during the War of Attrition, 1969. The .50cal. Browning heavy machine gun, locally manufactured, is still standard Israeli issue. (Author's collection)

show-down, urged Egypt to use its new strength. Yielding to these promptings, Nasser moved 100,000 men and 1,000 tanks up into the Sinai. Buoyed up by a sense of mission as the war leader of the Pan-Arabic cause which obsessed him, and by confidence in his new Russian-supplied equipment, he demanded the withdrawal of the UN force which had separated the Israelis and

Communications post during night manoeuvres in the 1960s–70s. Note Uzi SMG and FN/FAL rifle. (Author's collection)

Egyptians since 1957. Then he again closed the Straits of Tiran, and in taunting broadcasts invited the Israelis to fight. The prospect for Israel was daunting. On its borders were half a million Arab soldiers, 700 modern aircraft and 2,000 tanks. Attack seemed imminent, not only by Israel's neighbouring Arab states but also by strong contingents from Saudi Arabia, Algeria, Iraq, Sudan and Kuwait.

Israel's only defence against annihilation was a pre-emptive strike. To be effective it had to be delivered with total surprise, so Israel deliberately gave the impression of being at ease. On Saturday 3 June 1967 newspapers carried photographs of Israeli soldiers on leave, relaxing with their families on the beaches. Dayan, as Defence Minister, made a masterly speech in which he conveyed the impression that war was not imminent. Chief-of-Staff Gen. Yitzhak Rabin looked no busier than usual.

The surprise Israeli air strike went in at 0745hrs on 5 June, when most Egyptian aircraft were on the ground and their pilots were at breakfast. By 1030hrs the Egyptian Air Force had virtually ceased to exist, and with it all chances of Arab victory. The Israeli planes then turned on Syria and Jordan, and destroyed their air cover as well.

Zahal's order of battle consisted of 21 brigades

Estimated Israeli Deployment
June 1967

Northern Command (Gen. Elazar). Committed on West Bank, some units later to Syrian front:
  Ugda (Gen. Peled):
    Armd.Bde. (Col. Ram)—one bn. Centurion, one bn. AMX-13
    Armd.Bde. (Col. Bar-Kochva)—three bns. Sherman, one bn.mech.inf.
    Inf.Bde.
Central Command (Gen. Narkiss). Committed Jerusalem sector:
    6th ('Etzioni') Inf.Bde. (Col. Amitai)
    10th ('Harel') Mech.Bde. (Col. Ben-Ari)—incl. mixed bn. Sherman, Centurion; one bn. AMX-13
    55th Airborne Bde. (Col. Gur)
    Inf.Bde. (Col. Shehem?)
    Inf.Bde. (Col. Yotvat?)
Southern Command (Gen. Gavish). Committed Sinai, some units later to Syrian front:
  Ugda (Gen. Tal):
    7th Armd.Bde. (Col. Gonen)—79th Tk.Bn., M48; 82nd Tk.Bn., Centurion
    Armd.Bde. (Col. Aviram)—one bn. Sherman, one bn. AMX-13
    202nd Airborne Bde. (Col. Eitan)
    Mech.Recce Task Force (Col. Barom)—incl.bn. M48, some AMX-13
  Ugda (Gen. Yoffe):
    Armd.Bde. (Col. Shadni)—two bns. Centurion
    Armd.Bde. (Col. Sela)—two bns. Centurion
  Ugda (Gen. Sharon):
    Armd.Bde. (Col. Zippori)—one bn. Centurion, one bn. Sherman
    Airborne Bde. (Col. Matt)
    Inf.Bde.
    Mech.Recce Bn.—AMX-13
  Independent (8th?) Armd.Bde. (Col. Mendler). Held back in Negev, covering Egyptian armoured reserve 'Shazli Force'.
Syrian Front, 9–10 June:
Units known to have taken part in storming the Golan Heights include:
    8th Armd.Bde. (Col. Mendler)—two bns. Sherman, one bn. mech.inf.
    Armd.Bde. (Col. Ram)—from West Bank/Samaria
    Armd.Bde. (Col. Bar-Kochva)—from West Bank/Samaria
    1st ('Golani') Inf.Bde.
    Airborne Bde. (Col. Matt)—from Sinai
    plus either three or four other infantry brigades, with integral tank support.

The crew of a Soltam L33 155mm SP howitzer pose with their equipment. They wear the fire-retardant Nomex overalls, and 'bone dome' helmets with integral radio equipment, which were issued to most Israeli armour crews by the Yom Kippur War. (Christopher F. Foss)

—nine armoured, three combined infantry and armoured, three paratroop (including one serving as mechanised infantry) and six infantry. Four armoured brigades would see service on more than one front.

At 0815hrs Gen. Israel Tal's armoured Ugda attacked the Egyptians entrenched at Rafah junction, led by Col. Shmuel Gonen's famous 7th Armoured Brigade. Tal's plan was to envelop the Egyptians by rolling up their defence from the flank through the main road from Gaza. His Pattons, Centurions and paratroopers overran the crossroads in stiff fighting, and struck out for El Arish. Under orders to keep going and not engage in duels, the 7th Brigade ran through the eight-mile-deep defences within a few hours. Recovering, the Egyptians blocked the road behind them with heavy artillery fire. Brig. Rafael Eitan led his paratroopers into close-quarter fighting with the Egyptian infantry. With the help of air support the Egyptians were broken, and Aviram's armoured brigade hurried to join the 7th. On the morning of 6 June El Arish was captured.

On the southern edge of the Sinai front—the Abu Ageila perimeter—Gen. Sharon's Ugda faced the Egyptian 2nd Division. Protected by artillery, minefields, wire, tanks and sand dunes, the deep Egyptian positions were a formidable barrier blocking the roads across the Sinai. Sharon sent a battalion of paratroopers behind the Egyptian lines by night to surprise the enemy artillery and put the guns out of action. This done, Sharon sent his infantry, supported by tanks and artillery, against the left flank of the Egyptian positions. By morning the route westwards to the Canal was open. Sharon's battle of Um Katef was one of the outstanding successes of the war. It showed that precise orchestration of fire and movement by infantry, tanks, artillery and heli-borne paratroopers was possible on a divisional scale *at night*, and vindicated the considerable effort Zahal had put into night combat training.

Gen. Abraham Yoffe's armoured Ugda achieved the 'impossible' by moving two Centurion brigades across trackless sand dunes. Thrusting westward to the south of Ugda Tal, the brigades of Shadni and Sela screened Tal's southern flank from Egyptian counter-attack, and ambushed units of the Egyptian 4th Division coming up

Border Police, dressed in their distinctive green berets and light grey tropical fatigues, search every yard of ground during an anti-terrorist patrol on the Jordanian front. (Author's collection)

from Jebel Libni. By mid-day on 6 June the Egyptian army in northern Sinai was virtually destroyed.

All that could save the survivors was retreat—but before they could reach and cross the Suez Canal they had to pull back through the strategic Mitla and Jidi passes. As fighting continued around Jebel Libni and Bir Gifgafa, Gen. Yoffe was ordered by the GOC Southern Command, Gen. Gavish, to send tanks in a breakneck drive to cut the Egyptians off from the passes. Col. Shadni's Centurion brigade made a forced march, dwindling steadily as tank after tank ran out of fuel. Only nine Centurions were still moving when they reached the Mitla Pass at 1800hrs on 6 June—and four of those were out of fuel and under tow! The handful of tanks, with some half-track infantry, dug in at the pass and awaited the arrival of the retreating enemy columns. Fierce fighting went on all night, but by dawn Sela's brigade had begun to come up in support, and Israeli aircraft were causing havoc among the tight-packed

columns of Egyptian transport. Literally thousands of burnt-out vehicles soon littered the desert roads. Those Egyptians who managed to escape did so on foot, swimming the Canal to safety.

The pre-arranged Jordanian targets in the expected destruction of Israel were Jerusalem, and an air force base on the Jezreel Plain. When Jordanian troops seized the former UN Headquarters building south-east of the city at mid-day on 5 June, the Israelis at once retaliated. Uri Ben-Ari's 10th ('Harel') Bde., a mechanised force with two tank battalions, made a rapid eastwards thrust north of the city, seizing the high ground and cutting the Ramallah–Jerusalem road; the Jordanian 60th Armd.Bde. was blocked from reinforcing their troops in the capital. Meanwhile, mechanised infantry units captured Latrun and pushed north-eastwards to Ramallah itself.

That night Col. Mordechai Gur's 55th Parachute Bde. attacked the Jordanian positions in the northern part of Jerusalem. Fierce hand-to-hand fighting ensued; the heaviest engagement took place at Ammunition Hill, where stubborn Jordanian defenders resisted the 66th Parachute Bn. to the last man and caused heavy casualties. Meanwhile the 6th ('Etzioni') Inf.Bde. fought its

Brig. Danny Matt, a much-wounded veteran of Israel's wars, commanded a parachute brigade in Sinai in 1967; the following year he led a daring 120-mile raid deep into Egypt. In 1973 it was his reserve parachute brigade which spearheaded Sharon's daring 'counter-crossing' of the Suez Canal, leading to the encirclement of the 3rd Egyptian Army. Here he wears the maroon paratroopers' beret with the badge of a general officer. (Author's collection)

Israel determined not to pass up a possible opportunity to seize once and for all the dominating Heights from which so many Syrian shells had fallen on the Israeli valley floor over many years. An attack was ordered on 9 June.

Gen. Elazar, GOC Northern Command, mounted several simultaneous infantry attacks along the Syrian border; prominent among the attackers were the élite 1st ('Golani') Bde., and four other infantry brigades were committed. Col. Mendler commanded an armoured brigade with Centurions and Shermans, and the armoured brigades of Ram and Bar-Kochva were brought up from the West Bank, where they had fought at Jenin and Nablus. The armoured thrusts were headed by bulldozers to clear minefields and obstacles. Very heavy losses were sustained as the tanks fought their way up slopes, sometimes with a one-in-eight gradient, under fire from dug-in defenders; the Sherman battalion of Mendler's brigade lost all but three tanks, and the Cen-

way into the southern part of the city. On the morning of 7 June Gur ordered his paratroopers into the attack on the Old City, lost to the Israelis since the 1948 campaign. By 1000hrs they had reached the Western Wall of the Temple, the holiest of Jewish holy places, and went on to capture the 'Etzion Bloc', Hebron and Bethlehem.

A third sector was opened up to the north, where Gen. Elazar sent the armoured brigades of Ram and Bar-Kochva from Ugda Peled to take Nablus and Jenin in Samaria. Within 24 hours Elazar's troops were on the Jordan, controlling the bridges: the West Bank had fallen. An Iraqi contingent which had been supposed to take part in the anticipated Arab victory had no chance to get into action.

Apart from continual artillery duels and some air activity the Syrian front had remained quiet during 5–8 June. There was a desire among the Israeli government not to antagonise unnecessarily the Soviet Union, whose favoured clients the Syrians were; there was also the stark military fact that most Israeli forces were engaged in the Sinai and the West Bank, and the Syrian defence positions along the commanding Golan Heights were formidably strong. Syria would have been willing for a cease-fire on 8 June; but in the event

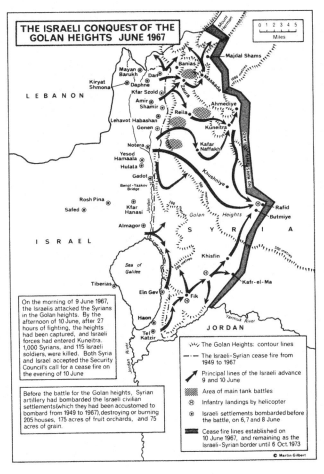

THE ISRAELI CONQUEST OF THE GOLAN HEIGHTS JUNE 1967

On the morning of 9 June 1967, the Israelis attacked the Syrians in the Golan heights. By the afternoon of 10 June, after 27 hours of fighting, the heights had been captured, and Israeli forces had entered Kuneitra. 1,000 Syrians, and 115 Israeli soldiers, were killed. Both Syria and Israel accepted the Security Council's call for a cease-fire on the evening of 10 June

Before the battle for the Golan heights, Syrian artillery had bombarded the Israeli civilian settlements(which they had been accustomed to bombard from 1949 to 1967), destroying or burning 205 houses, 175 acres of fruit orchards, and 75 acres of grain.

⟋⟋⟋ The Golan Heights: contour lines

—·— The Israeli-Syrian cease fire from 1949 to 1967

→ Principal lines of the Israeli advance 9 and 10 June

▨ Area of main tank battles

Ⓗ Infantry landings by helicopter

Ⓧ Israeli settlements bombarded before the battle, on 6, 7 and 8 June

▰▰ Cease fire lines established on 10 June 1967, and remaining as the Israeli-Syrian border until 6 Oct. 1973

© Martin Gilbert

Zahal half-tracks move across the desolate Golan plateau during the Yom Kippur War. Seconds after this photo was taken the infantry section came under fire and the photographer was wounded. (Author's collection)

turions suffered bad casualties. But after just 27 hours the Golan Heights were captured; Bar-Kochva's Shermans held Kuneitra, the main town on the Heights, just 30 miles from Damascus, and Syria appealed to the UN for a cease-fire.

One reason for the rapid victory over the main enemy, Egypt, lay in Gen. Tal's standing orders to his tank officers. Tanks must continue to fight and advance towards the objective, no matter if command was lost, if tanks found themselves out of contact or if there was doubt about the general situation. In the advance on El Arish, Col. Gonen's tank force failed to remain concentrated, 79th Tank Bn.'s Pattons 'lost' the paratroop force they were escorting, a lead battalion was cut off and running out of fuel and ammunition, and the reserve brigade spent the first critical day out of action in the sand dunes. Yet Tal's tanks reached their Stage One objective, El Arish, in 12 hours rather than the planned 24 hours. On the way they defeated ten infantry battalions, five tank battalions and four artillery regiments, largely because commanders did not pause to re-organise or search for their mother formations. Tal had the foresight to realise that regrouping would happen automatically when the various elements came together at El Arish.

Throughout the war the rate of advance of the armoured columns was speeded up by parachuting fuel and water ahead.

The war cost Israel 777 dead and 2,586 wounded, with 17 men, mostly pilots, taken prisoner. The Arabs had more than 15,000 dead or wounded and lost 12,000 as prisoners. They had also lost 1,000 tanks, 452 planes, practically all their equipment and 26,000 square miles of territory. The margin of the Israeli victory was astonishing; but the overwhelming victory did not produce the long period of calm they had hoped for. Within a very short period the Soviet Union had replaced 70 per cent of Egypt's materiel losses, while on the other fronts terrorist activity increased.

The War of Attrition

The extraordinary Israeli victory of 1967 attracted many foreign observers to Israel. Some marvelled at the absence of parade-ground discipline and military ceremonial in the Army yet noticed that the part-time soldiers often showed greater proficiency than the regulars in many advanced countries. A former British brigadier wrote that every Israeli soldier 'knew the main elements of his job, which he carried out with dispatch, rigorous self-discipline and amazing efficiency'. The Israelis, he said, were 'the toughest, most reliable, most aggressive, most indefatigable' fighters in the world.

After the Six-Day War rank structure changed with the introduction of the 'Tat-Aluf' between colonel and general ranks; Tat-Aluf became the equivalent to brigadier, and Aluf (the rank held by Ugda commanders) became equivalent to major-general.

A number of changes were made in the Israeli armour inventory. The AMX-13, by now clearly outclassed, was withdrawn from front-line service in all but reconnaissance units. A programme of replacing the vulnerable open-hull M3 half-tracks with completely enclosed M113s was begun. A drive to standardise fuel and ammunition types led to the refitting of the whole M48 Patton and Centurion force with Continental diesel engines and British L7 105mm guns. From 1970 numbers of new M60A1 tanks were received from the USA, as were M107 and M109 SP guns. Despite obviously greater difficulties, quantities of the T-54 and T-55 tanks captured in 1967 were modified to bring them partly into line with Israeli requirements, and put into service. There was no urgent need to replace the 105mm Sherman in those units which still had it—the venerable design had stood up well in battle with M47s and M48s in 1967, and would no longer be committed to first-line combat.

The Israelis had captured a number of Soviet PT-76s, the light amphibious tank used as a reconnaissance vehicle, as well as armoured personnel carriers BTR-40, BTR-50 and BTR-152. Some of these, with modifications, were brought into use. A particularly useful acquisition was the Russian M-54 130mm gun, which has a range of about 17 miles. The Israelis used this weapon against terrorist targets in Jordan. The B-24 240mm rocket launchers and 120 and 160mm mortars were also used. Among small arms, the excellent AK-47 assault rifle had been captured in large numbers, and some Israeli units were wholly equipped with it.

As the Egyptians re-armed after 1967 they brought up an immense number of heavy guns to pound the Israeli positions, and on the Canal front fighting was intermittent. Zahal built a chain of strong observation points from Port Fuad in the north to Suez in the south. This chain became known to journalists as the 'Bar-Lev Line', after the Chief-of-Staff, but it was not the type of fortification that the label implies. Even at its strongest it was little more than a series of small strongholds to provide shellproof shelter for look-outs and patrols. The 40 posts along the entire

M60A1 tank in Sinai, 1973. Generally satisfactory, it suffered from one vulnerability which had to be remedied urgently after the October War. The fast turret traverse system tended, if hit, to spray hydraulic fluid with a low flashpoint into the tank, causing explosive internal fires. (Author's collection)

length of the Canal were never all manned at the same time as the total garrison was 400 men. The line's strength lay in its mobile artillery and tank support.

In March 1969 (by Israeli official dating) a fourth real war developed between Israel and Egypt—the War of Attrition—a bloody, wearing and expensive war that raged on both sides of the Canal. For the first time Zahal was compelled to wage war from static lines along the borders. 'Digging in' became the main task: the Army had never used as much as barbed wire, mines, concrete and sandbags before. The change stimulated the development of various electronic devices, including electronic fences. The heavy Egyptian bombardment taught that sandbags did not provide adequate shelter for soldiers. Israeli army engineers constructed bunkers and trenches, and even pulled up the railway tracks that crossed the Sinai to strengthen these emplacements. Soviet manuals provided the best instruction on the proper method of construction and reinforcement for bunkers.

In one barrage it was estimated that the Egyptians fired more than 10,000 shells in a few hours. Without the artillery strength to reply in kind to the Egyptians, the Israelis resorted to what they did best—raids and surprise attacks. In this, too, they conformed to their basic doctrine that the war must be taken to the enemy.

One of the earliest deep-penetration raids was against a transformer station about 250 miles north of the Aswan Dam. The raiders blew up the station and some bridges, and so shocked Egyptians that for several weeks their artillery was silent. On the next occasion, paratroops and marine commandos raided Green Island and demolished the radar and anti-aircraft guns. Then came the ten-hour 40-mile 'run-wild' raid at Ras-Saafrana, Gulf of Suez, when the marauders destroyed 20 Egyptian installations. Once again, the Egyptians stopped shelling the Israeli positions along the Canal. At Sheduan Island, in the Red Sea, paratroopers blew up the radar station and fortifications.

The most spectacular raid occurred on 26 December 1969. Russian technicians had set up a sophisticated radar station to guard the western bank of the Gulf of Suez. Zahal sent in a helicopter-borne task force of electronics experts protected by paratroopers. Landing in the dark, the paratroops quickly overran the radar base; then, directed by the experts, they dismantled or cut away the radar equipment with acetylene torches. Helicopters lifted this heavy booty back to the Israeli side of the Gulf.

The situation became politically critical, and the Russians persuaded the Egyptians to accept an American cease-fire proposal on 7 August 1970. Thus ended the War of Attrition. Including the 'official' duration of the war, there had been 1,141 days of inconclusive warfare on Israel's three fronts. The Israelis lost a total of 367 killed and 999 wounded on the Egyptian front between June 1967 and January 1970. On all fronts the total was 721 Israelis killed in battle or terrorist incursions, with 2,659 wounded. The Egyptians lost 300 men a day at the height of the War of Attrition.

The October War

Israel's continued success in war is to a large extent due to its astonishingly successful reserve army mobilisation system. After service in the regular Army—as a professional or as a conscript —all men and many women become part of the reserve. In the first line are men aged 21 to 39; in the second line are those aged 39–44. During periods of crisis the upper age limit is raised to 55 for men and 36 for women. Reservists must serve for a month each year—and the service is *active*.

Some reservist units are at almost full strength, others are half-strength and others have only a cadre, depending on their degree of 'liability to fight'. In an emergency, individuals and small groups are called up by codes over the radio or flashed on the television and cinema screens. They include such phrases as: 'Smooth shave', 'Deep roots', 'Sabras', 'Electric toaster', 'Harry and friends', 'Sweet life' and 'Baseball bat'.

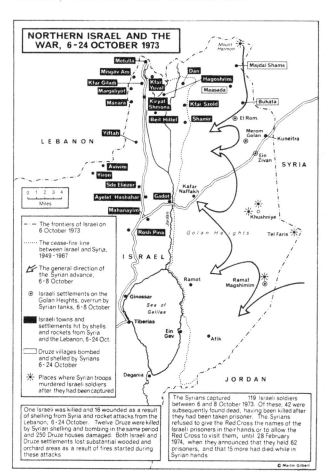

NORTHERN ISRAEL AND THE WAR, 6-24 OCTOBER 1973

- · - · - The frontiers of Israel on 6 October 1973
- ········· The cease-fire line between Israel and Syria, 1949 - 1967
- The general direction of the Syrian advance, 6 - 8 October
- ⊛ Israeli settlements on the Golan Heights, overrun by Syrian tanks, 6 - 8 October
- ■ Israeli towns and settlements hit by shells and rockets from Syria and the Lebanon, 6 - 24 Oct.
- ☐ Druze villages bombed and shelled by Syrians 6 - 24 October
- ✳ Places where Syrian troops murdered Israeli soldiers after they had been captured

One Israeli was killed and 16 wounded as a result of shelling from Syria and rocket attacks from the Lebanon, 6 - 24 October. Twelve Druze were killed by Syrian shelling and bombing in the same period and 250 Druze houses damaged. Both Israeli and Druze settlements lost substantial wooded and orchard areas as a result of fires started during these attacks

The Syrians captured 119 Israeli soldiers between 6 and 8 October 1973. Of these, 42 were subsequently found dead, having been killed after they had been taken prisoner. The Syrians refused to give the Red Cross the names of the Israeli prisoners in their hands, or to allow the Red Cross to visit them, until 28 February 1974, when they announced that they held 62 prisoners, and that 15 more had died while in Syrian hands

© Martin Gilbert

Estimated Israeli Deployment
October 1973

Given the existing security limitations; the confused nature of the fighting, in which units were gathered into *ad hoc* formations on a temporary basis and later deployed to other formations or another front; and the conflicting versions of the facts published by Arab and Israeli sources, the following notes are obviously fragmentary and highly speculative in some cases:

Northern Command (Gen. Hofi)

36th Mechanised Ugda (Gen. Eitan):
 188th ('Barak') Armd.Bde.
 7th Armd.Bde.
 1st ('Golani') Inf.Bde.
 31st Airborne Bde.

146th Armd. Ugda (Gen. Peled):
 9th Armd.Bde.
 19th Armd.Bde.
 20th Armd.Bde.
 70th Armd.Bde.

240th Armd. Ugda (Gen. Laner):
 By 10-10-73:
  19th Armd.Bde. (ex-146th Ugda)
  79th Armd. Bde.
  20th Armd.Bde. (ex-146th Ugda)
  17th Armd.Bde.
  14th Inf.Bde.?

Southern Command (Gen. Gonen)

252nd Armd. Ugda (Gen. Mendler kia;
  Gen. Magen):
 14th Armd.Bde. (Col. Reshev)
 401st Armd.Bde. (Col. Shomron)
 460th Armd.Bde. (Col. Amir)
 Inf.Bde.
143rd Armd.Ugda (Gen Sharon):
 421st Armd.Bde.
 14th Armd.Bde. (ex-252nd Ugda)
 55th Airborne Bde. (Col. Matt)
 Armd.Bde.
 Inf.Bde.

162nd Armd. Ugda (Gen. Adan):
 217th Armd.Bde. (Col. Karem)
 600th Armd.Bde. (Col. Baram)
 460th Armd.Bde. (ex-252nd Ugda)
 202nd Airborne Bde.
 Inf.Bde.
Plus, at some point:
146th Composite Ugda (ex-Syrian front?):
 Inf.Bde.
 Mech.Bde.
440th Composite Ugda (ex-Syrian front?):
 Three inf.bdes.

From an assembly point reservists are hurried to their units in batches. Small permanent cadres keep heavy equipment—tanks, self-propelled guns, bridge-layers—maintained and ready for use. In launching their 1973 invasion of Israel the Arab leaders over-estimated the time Israel needed to mobilise its reserves. The error was fatal.

Nevertheless, the IDF also failed. It was caught by surprise when the attack was made at 1400hrs on 6 October, the Holy Day of Atonement—Yom Kippur—when a large part of the population spends the entire day in prayer. The key element of the contingency plan was that the Intelligence services would provide at least 48 hours' advance warning. In fact, warnings *were* given by Zahal officers, but they were ignored. Thus military units were at low strength and some had stood down completely.

As mobilisation began the situation was so critical that officers stood in the assembly camps putting together tank crews as men arrived; a gunner, loader, driver and tank commander who might never have served together would be made into a crew and sent into action straight off the march. Many reservists drove to the Syrian front in their own cars. One reservist, on business in Geneva, returned to Tel Aviv airport in his private plane and was redirected to a small strip close to the Syrian front.

The war, lasting almost three weeks, can be divided into four major phases. It began with a desperate holding phase, 6–7 October, and continued with only partially successful counter-attacks on 8–10 October. Then came the Israeli offensive against Syria, complemented by the repulse of an Egyptian armoured assault on 11–14 October. The last stage was the continued Israeli offensive in Egypt on 15–25 October.

The Syrian Front

The attack opened with damaging air raids by Syrian Sukhoi fighter-bombers. The Syrians then advanced on the Golan Heights on a wide front, with the 5th, 7th and 9th Inf. Divs. leading—each with some 200 tanks under command—and the 1st and 3rd Armd. Divs. and several independent brigades following them, ready to exploit local success. In all the Syrians fielded some 1,260 tanks. Facing them on the 'Purple Line' Defences were one Israeli infantry brigade, the 188th ('Barak') Armd. Bde. with about 100 tanks and 44 SP guns; and parts only of the famous 7th Armd. Bde., whose full strength was some 105 tanks. The 7th held a line from the Lebanese border to Kunietra; the 188th, a front of 40km (of much easier tank country) from Kuneitra south to the Jordanian border. The Israeli tankers were thus immediately outnumbered three to one, and at some points during the battle which followed the odds would be 12 to one.

Over a battlefield which the Israelis later called 'The Valley of Tears' the 7th Armd. Bde. bought time for the reservists to be mustered. The Syrians did not have the walk-over they expected. The Israelis had prepared 'tank ramps' from which the tank guns had ranged in on every feature of the plateau. They took heavy toll of the mine-clearing and bridge-laying tanks which led the Syrian advance; but the mass of enemy armour, supported by very heavy artillery fire from 1,300 guns, could not be stopped, and rolled through the ditches and minefields. In the north the 7th, aided by rougher terrain, managed to counter-attack with some success, holding its positions during night battles; but in the south the 188th Armd. Bde. was overrun. By dawn on 7 October Syrian units overlooked Israeli towns on the Sea of Galilee.

That the reserves arrived in an orderly way, ready for battle, was largely the work of Maj. Gen. Dan Laner, a reserve paratroop officer. Hurrying from his kibbutz, he set up a command post at Arik Bridge, and from there he put tanks into units as and when they arrived, and sent them up on to the hills. In all, four reserve armoured brigades—the 79th, 14th, 17th and 19th—were rushed up to plug the gap in the 'Purple Line', entering battle squadron by squadron as available. By nightfall on 7 October the front was stabilising. Laner's handling of the crisis proved that the reservists system worked.

The continued success of the 7th Armd. Bde. in holding the northern sector led to it being left to get on with the job while attention was concentrated on sealing and reversing the Syrian breakthrough near Rafid. Thus it was that by 9 October the exhausted survivors of this superb unit were at the point of collapse. At the last moment some 13 tanks of the rebuilt 188th Bde. arrived to support them, throwing back the latest Syrian attack. Just seven tanks of the 7th Bde.'s original 105 were still running. For four days the brigade had held off repeated attacks by vastly greater forces, and had destroyed some 460 enemy AFVs.

On 10 October the reinforced 7th and 188th Armd. Bdes. led an Israeli counter-offensive north of Kuneitra, and Laner's 19th, 20th and 79th Armd. Bdes. advanced in the south. A great salient was forced into the Syrian lines, bringing Israeli guns within range of Damascus. On 13 October the Israelis severely punished a counter-attack by the Iraqi 3rd Armd. Division. The Jordanian 40th Armd. Bde., attacking on the Iraqis' left flank, were hit hard on the 16th and 18th. This was the last major clash in an armoured confrontation which cost the Syrians and their allies a total of some 1,200 AFVs—though at heavy cost to the Israelis. The symbol of victory on this front was the recapture of Mt. Hermon in a joint assault by paratroopers and the 'Golani' Bde.

The Egyptian Front

Here the assault began in a different way. First came a heavy but brief artillery bombardment, followed by attacks by some 150 MiGs on Israeli air bases, command posts, supply dumps and communications centres. Barrages of SAM missiles prevented the Israeli Air Force from intervening with its usual effectiveness. On the afternoon of 6 October, while the lightly-held Bar-Lev Line was blanketed by artillery fire, amphibious assault

1: Hagana infantryman, 1948
2: Jeep recce. trooper, IDF 5th Bde.; Negev, October 1948
3: Tank driver, 82nd Tank Bn.; Faluja sector, late 1948

A

1: Colonel, Armoured Corps staff, late 1950s
2: Paratrooper, 202nd Airborne Bde.; Mitla Pass, October 1956
3: Infantryman, 27th Mechanised Bde.; Sinai, October 1956

B

1: Infantryman, 6th ('Etzioni') Bde.; Jerusalem, June 1967
2: Sergeant, 79th Tank Bn., 7th Armoured Bde.; Sinai, June 1967
3: Paratrooper, 55th Airborne Bde.; Jerusalem, June 1967

C

1: 2nd Lieutenant, Training Command, 1970s
2: Female recruit, 1970s
3: 1st Lieutenant, 202nd Airborne Bde., 1970s

D

1: 1st Lieutenant, Armoured Corps, 1973
2: Infantryman, Syrian front, 1973

E

1: Staff Colonel, *c.*1950
2: Lieutenant-General, 1960s
3: Major-General, 1967

4: Corporal, Border Police, 1960s-70s
5: Nahal girl soldier, 1960s-70s

1: Corporal, 1st ('Golani') Inf. Bde., 1970s
2: Warrant Officer, Artillery, 1970s
3: Captain, 7th Armoured Bde., 1970s
4: Sergeant parachute rigger, 202nd Airborne Bde., 1970s
5: Recruit, Armoured Corps, 1970s

G

1: Infantryman, Golan Heights, late 1970s
2: Paratroop officer, 1980s
3: Infantryman, West Bank, 1981

2

1

3

H

teams in APCs and assault boats crossed the Canal at several points. Numerous 'tank-hunter' squads screened the landing of the heavier troops who followed; these were hand-picked infantry lavishly armed with RPG-7 rocket launchers and two-man wire-guided Malyutka ('Sagger') anti-tank missiles. The assault commandos used high-pressure hoses to wash great gaps in the high sand ramparts bulldozed up along the banks by the Israelis; Russian pontoon bridges were then laid at these points, and heavy troops began to cross into the bridgeheads. Their immediate opposition totalled some 1,000 Zahal men and 90 tanks.

The first counter-attacks by Gen. Mendler's 252nd Armd. Ugda (14th, 401st Reserve and 460th Reserve Armd. Bdes.) were repulsed with high losses by the 'tank-hunters', largely due to the failure of 1967-type 'armoured charge' tactics inadequately supported by mechanised infantry; by the afternoon of 7 October the division had lost some 200 of its 300 tanks. By this point some 40,000 Egyptian troops—five divisions—were on the east bank, with 800 tanks, holding a strip of desert eight miles deep. SAM batteries continued to prevent serious interference by the Israeli Air Force.

Under overall command of Lt. Gen. Bar-Lev, the Suez front was divided into the North, Central and Southern sectors, commanded respectively by Gens. Adan, Sharon and Mendler (later killed in action). Counter-attacks on 8 October were repulsed, with further heavy losses suffered by 'Bren' Adan's 167th Armd. Ugda near Kantara, the Chinese Farm, and Fridan—the three brigades were reduced to a total of 120 tanks by that night. Sharon's 143rd Armd. Ugda suffered smaller casualties attacking the Chinese Farm on the 9th.

The scales began to tilt in Israel's favour on 14 October, when the anticipated Egyptian attempt to break out into central Sinai through the passes was met by the superior gunnery of hull-down Zahal tanks. The Egyptians launched five mechanised columns totalling some 1,000 tanks on a 90-mile front. They soon outran their supporting infantry, and—out from under the SAM umbrella at last—faced Zahal in a classic tank-vs-tank battle. In the largest tank battle since 1945 the Egyptians lost some 460 AFVs, against 40 Israeli tanks knocked out.

Now occurred the most audacious move of the war. Seizing the strategic initiative on the night of 15/16 October, Gen. 'Arik' Sharon pushed paratroopers and seven tanks across to the west bank of the Canal at Deversoir at the northern end of the Great Bitter Lake, using pontoon bridging equipment and existing hard-points. Fierce fighting took place meanwhile on the southern sector of the Chinese Farm positions held by the Egyptian 21st Armd. and 16th Inf. Divs. in order to secure the crossings against interference. It was only with difficulty that Danny Matt's paratroopers were reinforced on the west bank by some M107 SP guns. Several other Israeli assaults were mounted on the east bank to occupy the enemy's attention, and both Sharon's and Adan's units were heavily engaged on the 16th and 17th, successfully destroying large numbers of Egyptian tanks. Zahal had learnt its lesson, and 'all arms' teams of tanks properly supported by infantry in M113 APCs and SP guns were employed.

Sharon's increasing forces on the west bank spread out on 17–19 October, wreaking havoc in the enemy rear areas. Missile sites were eliminated, allowing Israeli Phantom jets to take a part in the battle. On the night of the 17th Adan's 162nd Armd. Ugda crossed the Canal, followed by the 252nd Armd. Ugda (led by Maj. Gen. Magen after Mendler's death) and the 14th and 421st Bdes. of Sharon's 143rd Ugda. Adan and Magen moved south to cut off the Egyptian 3rd Army, while Sharon swung north towards Ismailia. The Egyptians made desperate attempts to destroy the Israeli bridges; a particularly fierce action was fought by 3rd Army units at Wadi Mabouk, where a small force of Magen's division repulsed attacks at odds of one to five, and destroyed nearly 100 tanks by point-blank firing from higher ground, supported by air strikes. Completely encircled, the Egyptian 3rd Army was only saved by a cease-fire agreement imposed by the 'superpowers' on 24 October.

The cease-fire found the Israelis occupying 600 square miles of Egypt west of the Canal, encircling the 3rd Army and holding some 9,000 other prisoners. Egypt held a strip five to seven miles deep along the entire east bank, apart from the Deversoir corridor; and had taken some 250 Israeli prisoners. On the Golan front Israel had

Lt.Gen. David Elazar, GOC Northern Front at the time of the capture of the Golan Heights in 1967, was Zahal Chief-of-Staff in 1973. For uniform notes, see commentary on Plate F2. (Author's collection)

Zahal since 1973

At planning level the war resulted in various changes. One was the decision to produce an Israeli-designed and Israeli-built tank, drawing on long combat experience of Middle East warfare and incorporating various features of specific importance to Zahal. The planning group, under Gen. Tal, formulated the requirements which have led to the appearance of Merkava ('Chariot').

Crew protection was considered paramount, given Israel's high losses among trained technical personnel in 1973, and her precarious manpower position. The engine would be positioned in the front of the tank, and the design must include ballistically-angled armour. It is not thought that the armour plate is actually of the composite or 'Chobham' type, as has been reported; it certainly offers protection against small shaped-charge missiles by the use of spaced armour, however.

Firepower is equally vital: Israeli tanks will normally be outnumbered, and must be able to hit hard, and first. Tal's group chose the proven British 105mm gun, and this was fitted to Merkava I, coupled with a laser range-finder and a fire-control computer. Late in 1977 the German 120mm gun was substituted for Merkava II. Top speed was not considered to be of great importance, and on past experience of fighting over loose sand and stony plains the Israelis selected the 900hp Teledyne-Continental V12 diesel engine. A powerplant giving 1,200hp was later substituted.

A good deal of speculation has appeared in the military press regarding the rear hull of Merkava, and no doubt deliberate 'misinformation' has played its part in this. It was suggested that on-board infantry would be carried to deal with 'tank-hunters', a theory which fails to convince if one studies both the tactical realities of tank warfare, and the dimensions of Merkava. The large rear access hatch is believed to be for rapid, palletised ammunition resupply in combat, and doubtless doubles as an escape hatch. Protection against NBC warfare conditions is thought to be designed into the tank.

To replace their Second World War vintage half-tracks Zahal acquired a total of some 3,000 M113 APCs. Many of the original inventory of

occupied 160 square miles of territory and held 268 Syrian prisoners; about 120 Zahal men had fallen into Syrian hands. In materiel, Egypt, Syria and Iraq had lost more than 1,300 tanks; Zahal lost about 840, though final Israeli control of the battlefields allowed many to be recovered and repaired. Arab air forces had lost 368 aircraft, two-thirds of them Egyptian, in air-to-air fighting; Israel lost 114, all but 20 of them to ground fire. Egyptian and Syrian sources list personnel casualties as totalling 19,000 killed and 51,000 wounded. Israel lost 606 officers—including one major-general, 25 colonels and 80 majors—and 6,900 men.

Yom Kippur ended in an Israeli victory; recovering from their initial setbacks, Zahal achieved a stunning counter-blow and finished the war holding more Syrian and Egyptian territory than before. But the 'Great Crossing', as the Egyptians call their return to the east bank, was a tremendous psychological coup for the Arabs—humiliated by their total rout in 1967—and its propaganda value was fully exploited. Sharon's 'counter-crossing' into the Egyptian rear areas may be seen as a return—after a momentary hesitation—to Zahal's normal tactical and psychological approach.

some 4,000 half-tracks will no doubt be sold abroad; but at the time of writing large numbers are still in use, and various locally improvised modifications continue to appear, including a tall, box-like, armoured rear hull compartment.

Few armies can have such a variety of equipment, but then, no modern army has experienced so many wars in which to acquire enemy equipment. Zahal's 3,000 or so tanks include some 1,000 Centurions, 650 M48s, 925 M60A1s, about 400 T-54/55s, 150 T-62s, and 200 Merkavas with more being delivered all the time. Zahal has some 65 PT-76 amphibious light recce tanks, and several thousand other AFVs such as AML-60, AML-90 and RBY armoured cars, and captured Soviet BTR and BRDM personnel carriers.

Artillery includes some 600 howitzers of 105mm and 155mm calibre, 60 of 175mm and 50 of 203mm. More than 1,000 mortars include 81mm, 120mm and 160mm tubes, many of them self-propelled. There are rocket-launchers of 122mm, 135mm and 240mm; American Lance and Israeli Wolf missiles serve alongside captured Soviet 'katyushas'. Anti-tank missiles include 'Sagger', Cobra, Dragon, TOW, and SS:11. In all, the Zahal SP artillery branch has tripled in strength since 1973. For air defence Israel has nearly 1,000 Vulcan/Chapparal 20mm cannon and a large stock of Redeye missiles. Total artillery strength has increased by some 30 per cent since 1973; total armoured strength by rather more than that.

Even after achieving peace with Egypt, Zahal is taking no chances. The mobilised ground forces comprise 50 brigades: 20 armoured, of which five are at full strength, one at half-strength, and 14 at cadre strength; nine mechanised infantry (four half-strength, five cadre strength); nine infantry (four at full strength, five cadre strength); seven artillery, and five parachute brigades, of which three are 'paratroop air-mobile'.

An infantry brigade has three battalions and supporting arms and services, including a reconnaissance company and an artillery battalion. Brigades do not have their own transport, which is supplied as needed and then returns to Transport Command. Armoured brigade organisation is flexible; a brigade may have three tank battalions or two tank and one mechanised infantry. Mechanised or armoured infantry brigades, all

Maj.Gen. Yitzhak ('Hacka') Hofi, GOC Northern Front in 1973. He had won his laurels in years of border fighting; now he led the Israeli drive towards Damascus. Above the ribbons of the 1948, 1956 and 1967 wars he wears 'advanced parachutist's' wings—the star denotes 50 jumps. (Author's collection)

equipped with APCs, consist of two infantry battalions and one tank battalion.

Tank battalions have an HQ squadron and three sabre squadrons; a squadron has 11 tanks and a battalion 35. The paratroop battalion has an HQ company and three rifle companies; each company has five platoons of 30–35 men, each led by an officer. The HQ company is practically as strong, since it acts as the battalion reserve.

The active-duty army rose after 1973 to 150,000 men, with 237,000 first-line reserves and 223,000 second-line, plus 5,000 in the Nahal militia and 4,500 border guards.

The Har-Zion Method

Zahal constantly tried to make its soldiers more proficient, and the tougher generals would like to see the fighting units 'Har-Zionised'. Moshe Dayan was the first to coin the term 'Har-Zionism' to describe the spirit and morale which he believed permeated the IDF after the Six-Day War. It comes from the name of Meir Har-Zion, a captain in Unit 101 and, according to Dayan,

Israel's best and bravest soldier. A big, energetic man, the kibbutz-reared Har-Zion worked his way up through the ranks, and took part in many operations in the 1950s. An advocate of the dictum that 'sweat saves blood', he introduced rigorous training methods for his men. Greatly distressed by the death of his sister, killed while fighting Jordanian Bedouin who ambushed her in the hills, Har-Zion made an unauthorised personal raid on the Bedouin camp and shot dead his sister's killers. He was in action in Gaza and on the Syrian frontier; then, in an attack on an Arab Legion post, he was shot in the throat and arm. After a protracted recovery he was declared 80 per

Armoured Corps soldier at his devotions during a lull in the Sinai fighting of 1973. Orthodox Jewish soldiers carry their prayer vestments in their pouches. (Author's collection)

cent disabled, but he served in a headquarters unit during the Sinai campaign of 1956.

By June 1967 Har-Zion was a farmer and a captain in the reserves. He could not hold a rifle, and nothing active was expected of him; but on the night of 5 June he turned up among Israeli paratroopers who were preparing for their assault on the Arab Legion troops holding the Old City. He had a bag of grenades, the only weapon he could use with one good hand. His colonel, 'Motta' Gur, gave him a command. His exploits are too numerous to be related here, but one episode is especially noteworthy.

An Arab sniper had taken up position on the roof of a house and was shooting Zahal men in the street below. He held up the Israeli attack for an hour, despite several attempts to knock him out. Har-Zion stalked the man through the dangerous streets, climbing walls and finally appearing on a roof, from where he sprang onto the sniper's roof and killed him—all with a paralysed hand. With Jerusalem secured, Har-Zion rushed off by himself to the Golan Heights, where he took part in the deciding battle on the last day of the war.

When men are called up, the examining officers do not expect to find all of them as tough or as military-minded as Meir Har-Zion. In fact, few men are turned away, because Israel cannot afford the luxury of choosing only the best human specimens. What would be regarded as grounds for exemption in most other armies—flat feet, colour blindness, fingers missing, or illiteracy—do not apply in Israel. Exemptions for women are much more common; the IDF inducts only the best-educated girls from high school because the work they will do requires a high degree of literacy.

The Israeli Army has not been content to follow the rules established by other armies, as shown by the matter of water discipline, the subject of rigorous training along traditional lines in most armies. On several occasions Zahal doctors sent three different battalions of paratroopers on a forced march through the desert to the shores of the Red Sea. The first battalion marched on a canteen of water a day; the second with as much water as each man wanted; the third was provided not only with water but with tea, coffee, soft drinks and light alcohol. On all occasions the second battalion made the best time and its members were invariably in better health. The experiment proved that a man cannot get used to drinking less—those who had their water rationed for a longer time succumbed first when cut off from water. This finding is contrary to the old idea that men trained to live and fight on a small quantity of water are somehow tougher and can stand the pace longer.

Again, Zahal experiments prove that a trained man can function responsibly without sleep 24 hours a day for several days; the key, Army doctors say, is trusting him to carry on. Zahal does not consider that a unit should be relieved before it has had over 50 per cent casualties.

But simple endurance is not the main qualification for promotion or even for acceptance into the regular full-time Army. Zahal officers are more interested in the way in which men react to testing situations. For instance, after a long day's march in the desert or mountains, a section of ten men might find that they are carrying rations for only eight men. Psychologists observe and analyse the reaction of the soldiers to this contrived situation. Heavy reliance is placed on such psychological evaluations, and teams of psychologists are stationed with each unit. Psychologists are expected to decide which individuals are most suited to serve as tank drivers or tank gunners. In infantry units a psychologist's advice will be sought on which soldier will be a good mortarman or machine-gunner.

A unique characteristic of the system of training and guidance in the Israeli Army is the multiplicity of realistic, even dangerous, exercises using live ammunition. The purpose is to bring the soldier as close as possible to combat conditions, and to prepare the reserve soldier to adapt to the sharp transition from the life of a civilian to that of a fighting soldier. Entering the Army, however, is not the traumatic experience it might be in other countries; virtually all boys and girls will have been members of Gadna (Youth Battalions). Rather like a prep school for the forces, Gadna trains its pupils in firearms, flying, drill, parachuting, physical fitness, marching and leadership.

Many young Israelis, on becoming eligible for the draft, volunteer for Noar Halutzi Lohem

Lt.Gen. Elazar and Minister of Defence Moshe Dayan, Israel's most famous soldier, confer at a Sinai command post during the crisis of the Yom Kippur War; Elazar wears a flak jacket complete with hand grenade. Both men were subject to criticism for Zahal's state of preparedness on 6 October. (Author's collection)

(Fighting Pioneer Youth)—known universally as Nahal. Nahal remains as the embodiment of Ben Gurion's dream of an army of farmer-fighters. It has been said that Nahal represents the best and most responsible elements of the citizen army, the people who inspire the others.

Nahal is a military corps without any element of compulsion. It has military training and duties, it does agricultural work in remote new border settlements, and it provides an extra dimension—pioneering and service for the nation—which suits the idealistically minded. Universally regarded as an élite, Nahal is the most unusual element of the IDF because it is not only constantly at the front, but it is also a social body. The basic military training at the Nahal Command Training Camp is severe and thorough. Nahal units have served as the spearhead units on several fronts in each of the major crises since 1951. During the Suez Campaign they were involved in the crucial breakthrough to Raffah, the capture of El Arish and the Mitla Pass. During the Six-Day War and Yom Kippur they were committed on the southern front and in the Golan.

In yet another respect the Israeli Army—with the naval and air services—is unique among armies. As well as its conventional military task it

Two famous divisional commanders of the 1973 Sinai campaign: left, Maj.Gen. 'Bren' Adan, GOC 162nd Reserve Armoured Ugda; and right, the tempestuous Maj.Gen. Ariel 'Arik' Sharon, GOC 143rd Reserve Armoured Ugda. (Author's collection)

has multiple educational rôles. Beyond its natural responsibility to its own members, the Army provides teachers—the majority of them young women—for schools in hundreds of towns and villages throughout the nation. Still in their military uniform, these soldier-teachers deal with all the basic subjects. Perhaps more than anything else they are teaching the values by which they live: self-discipline and national service.

The Plates

A1: Hagana infantryman, 1948

Photos of the War of Independence show Hagana personnel in an indescribable variety of clothing; surplus British and US Army items were the norm, acquired piecemeal and worn with civilian additions. This typical Hagana fighter wears a British helmet and battledress blouse, civilian trousers, a US webbing rifle belt without braces and adorned with Mills grenades, and a British cotton clip bandolier. The weapons are the reliable British

.303 SMLE, and the PIAT anti-tank projector; some dozens of the latter represented Hagana's only realistic defence against Arab armour.

A2: Jeep reconnaissance trooper, IDF 5th Brigade; Negev, October 1948

The 5th ('Givati') Bde. was one of the formations committed to the relief of the northern Negev settlements. Some striking successes were recorded by fast reconnaissance units, typically mounted in jeeps fitted with MG34 machine guns. Various British and American surplus khaki drill clothing was worn; the matching field cap, with attached neck-flap and cloth chinstrap, was a home-grown Israeli innovation, widely seen in Hagana and the IDF in 1948–49. Note the *shemagh* headdress worn round the neck as a dust-scarf; today popularly associated with the Arabs only, it was quite widely worn by Israelis of the late 1940s.

A3: Tank driver, 82nd Tank Battalion; Faluja sector, late 1948

This jaunty figure is taken from a photo of the driver of '211', one of the two Cromwell tanks of the battalion's 'English Company'. His knitted cap-comforter and battledress trousers are British, as is the web belt and the holster modified to take the old 'broomhandle' Mauser; the USAAF surplus M1941 field jacket still bears the original shoulder patch.

B1: Colonel, Armoured Corps staff, late 1950s

The former Canadian Army officer, Lt.Col. Ben Dunkelman, who took command of the half-track-equipped 7th Bde. for Operation 'Hiram' in October 1948, and later retained command when it became the IDF's single regular armoured unit, wanted his men to present a smart, 'Second World War' appearance. He chose a green beret for his tank crews, and obtained private supplies of Canadian Army surplus berets; but shortly afterwards the authorities decreed that the regulation beret would be black. The 7th Bde. obeyed with reluctance, and today an original green Armoured Corps beret is a collector's item. No official Corps cap badge was worn until 1952; initially in white metal and later in dark bronze, it depicts a tank in a wreath above a scroll, and is worn pinned through a red cloth patch.

The Armoured Corps does not have a distinctive uniform, wearing the same olive green fatigues as the rest of the Army. During the 1950s green and black were designated as Corps colours; well-blackened boots are an Armoured Corps affectation, and in the 1950s many officers wore dark green scarves. The Corps shoulder patch, adopted after the 1956 War, is worn here in characteristic Zahal fashion, on a removable tab from the end of the left shoulder strap; it is a square of diagonal black and green stripes. The three leaves of a colonel—Aluf-Mishne—are worn in dark bronze, pinned through red cloth patches on both shoulder straps. The silver parachute 'jump-wings' are worn by almost all Zahal officers, as it is normally a required qualification; pale blue cloth backing indicates that no combat jumps have been made. Below the brevet are the ribbons of the 1948 and 1956 campaigns. The tank helmet is the Czech type worn for a time in the 1950s.

B2: Paratrooper, 202nd Airborne Brigade; Mitla Pass operation, October 1956
The few photos actually taken during this operation show a rimless British-style paratrooper helmet with forked chinstraps and string netting; a three-quarter-length jump-smock very similar in outline to the British Denison, but apparently in plain dark olive; and olive fatigue trousers with brown jump-boots. Some photos show the smock to be collarless, others shown an attached hood. The parachute rigs were US Army surplus, with main back and reserve chest packs. The Uzi submachine gun had its combat debut in this operation, but many of the paratroopers still carried the old Czech-made Mauser Kar 98k rifle.

B3: Infantryman, 27th Mechanised Bde., Sinai, October 1956
Photos of infantry in this campaign show a motley collection of clothing and equipment—as, indeed, do photos of reservist infantry in 1967. The 'kibbutz' sun-hat is popular throughout Israel, and is often seen in front-line photos of 1956; it is made in any number of light colours. British helmets of both patterns, American helmets and cap-comforters were all worn in the Sinai. Khaki drill fatigues are worn here with a mixture of British and US Army webbing items. The Czech-made Kar 98k was still in use in 1967.

C1: Infantryman, 6th ('Etzioni') Bde.; Jerusalem, June 1967

An American-style helmet is worn with olive fatigues, and a mixture of US and British surplus and Israeli-made webbing of similar design. A khaki-drill bush hat is slung on the back of the knapsack, its cloth chin-tapes around the US-pattern entrenching spade. The weapon is the heavy-barrel model of the FN/FAL series, used as the standard Zahal squad light automatic at this date. Note that the helmet is covered with both sacking and a string net; and that the bush hat is of the French pattern, often worn 'cowboy fashion' with the brim held up on both sides by knotting the tapes above the crown.

Lt.Gen. Elazar inspecting the Sinai battleground from a helicopter, October 1973. Battered armour litters a desert criss-crossed by tank tracks, and in the distance a knocked-out tank blazes. (Author's collection)

C2: Sergeant, 79th Tank Bn., 7th Armoured Bde.; Sinai, June 1967

A young Patton commander of 'Ugda Tal', carrying the folding-butt Uzi which is the IDF tankman's normal personal weapon, and the coloured signal-flags which are still widely used. The headgear is an Israeli modification of the old US Army pierced crash helmet, with added mike-boom. The tank suit illustrated was not very widely worn; many crews fought in the universal olive fatigue dress. The overall apparently caught fire easily, and the design of its zip fasteners hindered quick removal. Ranking was worn on cloth slip-over loops on the shoulder straps by officers, and on the sleeve—often temporarily pinned, as here—by NCOs like this sergeant (Samal). Tankmen rarely wore any equipment other than a belt and canteen.

C3: Paratrooper, 55th Airborne Bde.; Jerusalem, June 1967

One of the fiercest actions of this campaign was the capture of Ammunition Hill from the

Jordanian 4th ('Prince Hassan') Inf.Bn. by the 66th Bn. of Col. Gur's 55th (Reserve) Airborne Bde. on 5–6 June; half the Israeli battalion became casualties, and the Jordanians fought literally to the last man. The helmet is unchanged since 1956. The combat fatigues are now French Army surplus camouflage pattern, often in mismatched sets giving a sharp contrast in tone between jacket and trousers; both airborne and infantry models of this uniform were worn indiscriminately within the brigade. The Israeli-made webbing includes magazine pouches for the Uzi.

D1: 2nd Lieutenant, Training Command, 1970s

The pale khaki drill three-pocket blouse and matching skirt worn with white socks and black shoes is the everyday warm-weather service dress of female personnel of all ranks. An alternative is a pocketless shirt with long sleeves worn rolled, tucked into matching slacks. The bonnet is of the same shape throughout the female services, but varies in colour; for most ground forces it is midnight blue, and here bears the General Service badge well forward on the left side (detail, top right). Rank bars of this grade—Segen-Mishne—are pinned through red patches on the shoulder straps. The Training Command shoulder patch (detail, top left) is worn on an olive drab tab from the left shoulder. The black whistle lanyard identifies an instructor; the silver sword-and-olive-branch pin on the left collar point marks graduation from Officer School.

D2: Female recruit, CHEN, 1970s

During the War of Independence women fought alongside men in combat units. This practice was phased out in the early 1950s: although they receive basic field and weapon training, and take responsibility for their own perimeter security with live ammunition, women are not intended to initiate combat involvement. Israeli girls do two years in CHEN (women's services) on completing school; after basic training they specialise in a wide variety of alternative skills in the fields of logistics, communications, electronics, and so on. Recently women were even admitted to the ranks of Armoured Corps tank instructors. This cold-weather outdoor uniform for heavy work consists

Paratrooper armed with the new 5.56mm Galil assault rifle during a raid into 'Fatahland' in southern Lebanon to flush out terrorists. The Galil is a fine rifle whose designer drew on Zahal's deep experience of many foreign weapons, including the AK-47. It has a folding butt, built-in bipod, integral grenade launcher, and two particularly 'soldier-proof' features: a beer-bottle opener designed into the butt, to stop Zahal men using the lips of the magazine with dangerous consequences, and the fact that only six parts need be handled during the field-strip procedure. (Author's collection)

of an olive fatigue cap and zippered jacket, a brown sweater, and the khaki drill shirt and slacks uniform. The double-buckle boots are not normal Zahal issue; and note also the respirator case, of the US Army model.

D3: 1st Lieutenant, 202nd Airborne Brigade, 1970s

Everyday warm-weather service dress worn by an officer of this élite formation, the first (and for most of its history the only) regular parachute unit. Neatly pressed olive fatigues are worn with the paratrooper's characteristic maroon beret and red-brown jump-boots. The beret bears the Infantry badge (detail, top centre) on a scarlet patch. The two bars of this rank—Segen—are pinned through red patches to the shoulder straps; they are semi-cylindrical in shape, of dark bronze finish, with an embossed olive branch down the centre of each. The red-backed paratrooper's qualification wings indicate combat jumps: below them are the campaign ribbons for the 1967 and 1973 wars. The 202nd Bde. patch is worn at the shoulder on the usual tab—a maroon shield bearing a black serpent with white eyes, fangs and wings.

E1 : 1st Lieutenant, Armoured Corps, 1973

This battle-weary tank officer, carrying his mapboard and dragging a plastic sack of cerise/yellow air and ground recognition panels, wears the current Zahal armoured crew overalls, in fire-retardant Nomex material. Note detail of zippers. The 'bone dome' CVC helmet with integral radio equipment is, like the overall, of US origin. In combat clothing Zahal officers wear ranking in the form of printed green shapes on light khaki slip-on shoulder strap loops. A grim detail is the wearing of the identity tags around the ankle rather than the neck. In 1973 so many tank commanders received fatal or mutilating wounds to the head and neck, due to fighting with their heads out of the cupola to spot the roving Arab

Paratroopers wait to move off after assembling on a DZ in the hills of southern Sinai. Most are armed with the American M16, but note that the section retains one FN/FAL with grenade launcher fitted, and one FN/MAG squad light machine gun. (Author's collection)

'tank hunter' teams, that this method was felt more effective.

E2 : Infantryman, Syrian front, 1973

The archetypal Israeli reservist soldier—though if anything, the hair is rather tame in this view! Religious Jews wear the yarmulke at all times. This soldier wears conventional combat fatigues and Israeli-made webbing equipment, and carries the FN/MAG light machine gun. The black rubber rim fitted to the US-style helmet holds the hessian and netting double cover in place. The white stripe, common but not universal, was seen in both 1967 and 1973; it appears to have no significance beyond quick identification. Crossed double chin-straps are not limited to paratrooper helmets. The Instamatic camera was a common sight in the front line; according to a veteran of this campaign, reservists often risked their lives for a snapshot! In the background, an artilleryman wears a US-made flak jacket; issue seems to have been limited to 'static' troops such as gun crews.

Details : left to right : Northern Command shoulder patch, Central Command, Southern Command. All are normally white on midnight blue, but

The new Israeli Merkava tank on the ranges; note excellent ballistic shape of hull and turret. The small profile of the rear hull clearly disproves one of the rumours about this tank—that it incorporated a rear compartment for carrying infantry. The large rear access hatch is now believed to be for loading palletised ammunition, though it no doubt doubles as an emergency escape hatch under some circumstances. (Author's collection)

olive drab is sometimes seen. Zahal is so organised that the three area commands are capable of continuing operations independently should part of the country be overrun.

F1 : *Staff Colonel, c.1950*
The first truly Israeli uniform item to appear was the field cap, here in a stiffened version, with the neck-flap neatly doubled and hooked up. The badge is that of the General Staff, worn by general officers and staff colonels; apart from the much smaller scroll it is essentially similar to that of the Infantry Corps, shown in detail on Plate D. The US Army surplus 'chino' shirt bears the three bronze vine leaves of this rank—Aluf-Mishne.

F2 : *Lieutenant-General, 1960s*
'Rav-Aluf' is the highest rank in Zahal, approximating to lieutenant-general but referred to simply as 'general'. This figure is taken from various different Zahal Chiefs-of-Staff, but is not meant to depict an individual. The khaki service dress cap, with brown leather peak and strap, is seldom seen in photos and appears to be limited, in practice, to staff personnel. The khaki battledress is the regulation winter service dress, worn with the shirt collar open in the traditional Israeli manner. The two leaves and crossed sword and olive branch of this rank are pinned through red patches to the shoulder straps. The cap bears the GHQ cap badge, the usual sword-and-olive-branch motif central in an open Star of David

above a scroll; this motif is repeated, in miniature and pinned through red patches, on the collar points. (Photos show that the cap badge is sometimes but not invariably backed with red.) The GHQ shoulder patch is the usual midnight blue and white circle; the motif combines the Army's sword-and-olive-branch, the Air Force wings and the Navy's anchor. Parachute jump-wings are worn above the ribbons of the 1948, 1956 and 1967 wars. Note that clasps are attached to the first of these, in the form of a miniature menora and the sword-and-branch motif: see several portrait photos reproduced in this book.

F3 : *Major-General, 1967*
The front-line appearance of a Zahal general, taken from photos of Maj.Gen. Gavish, the commander of the Sinai front in 1967. The general's cap badge is worn on his personal beret in Infantry khaki. Note printed green-on-khaki-drill shoulder strap loops of rank; and plastic name tag above pocket.

F4 : *Corporal, Border Police, 1960s–70s*
The Border Police are a separate service, but have seen so much action against terrorists that their

Lt.Gen. 'Raful' Eitan commanded the battalion dropped at Mitla in 1956; led the mechanised parachute brigade within Ugda Tal in the 1967 Sinai campaign; and held a sector command on the Golan Heights in 1973. At the time of writing he is Zahal Chief-of-Staff. He wears the General Headquarters badge on his paratrooper's maroon beret; dark metal rank insignia on red backing patches on shoulder strap loops; 'advanced parachutist' wings in silver on the red backing indicating a combat jump; dark blue and white pilot's wings; and the ribbons of the Ot Haoz (Israel's second highest gallantry decoration) and 1973 War, above those of the 1948, 1956 and 1967 wars.

inclusion in this book is more than justified. They are distinguished by a shirt-and-slacks summer uniform in a light greyish shade of drill, the shirt of which is worn with the khaki battledress of winter uniform. Their green beret bears a silver badge; and, interestingly, the old British-style rank chevrons are retained, on both sleeves. Photos taken shortly after the Six-Day War show patrols in captured Russian BTR-152 APCs; their web equipment is camouflage-painted with green streaks.

F5: Nahal girl soldier, 1960s–70s
Nahal, whose special nature and function are described in the body of the text, have provided combat units in all Israel's wars; thus the Infantry cap badge and red backing. The shoulder patch is that of Nahal as a whole, rather than a brigade; it shows a white sword-and-sickle motif flanked by green boughs on a midnight blue diamond. The uniform is in other respects exactly as Plate D1.

G1: Corporal, 1st ('Golani') Infantry Brigade, 1970s
The NCO rank bars—here, those of Rav-Turai—are worn on both sleeves, high at the front. Above them on the left is the tab bearing the patch of this élite brigade. The beret is the khaki Infantry Corps model, with the Corps cap badge pinned through red cloth. On his left pocket is a red-backed badge indicating graduation from a Commando course—a dagger, point to the right, on a sunburst. On his right pocket, and more clearly shown on Plate G3, is an upright sword on red-enamelled flames, the Active Combat badge.

Nothing and nobody can make an Israeli soldier look smart . . . an infantryman relaxes in a tented camp, his Galil close to hand. The right wrist ID bracelet is official issue. (Author's collection)

G2: Warrant Officer, Artillery, 1970s

G2: Warrant Officer, Artillery, 1970s

The senior WO rank, Rav-Samel-Rishon, is identified by a rank badge of a sword-and-branch in a Star of David in a wreath; in shirtsleeve order it is worn on a right wrist strap, in the British Army fashion, and is backed with red. The Artillery Corps wears a black beret with a badge which closely resembles the Armoured Corps insignia apart from the central motif of a gun; most artillery units in Zahal are highly mobile or self-propelled, and operate close up with the tanks. The patch should logically be that of a brigade, and its red-and-black colours and crossed silver cannons suggest a specifically artillery affiliation. The ribbons of the 1956, 1967 and 1973 wars are worn. Typical badges on the flap of his right pocket would be the diamond-shaped silver award for Service in Occupied Territory, and the flaming sword of Active Combat.

G3: Captain, 7th Armoured Brigade, 1970s

The three bars of a Seren are worn through red patches on the shoulder straps; the Armoured Corps badge, through red on the black Corps

There is little formal ceremonial in Zahal, but on occasion unit flags are paraded. These artillerymen, who carry Uzis as personal weapons, are marching into a camp in Galilee. The placard at the rear is an enlargement of the Artillery Corps cap badge, the scroll bearing that title; the flanking flags appear to be in plain red and black, the corps colours. (Author's collection)

beret; and the brigade patch of this élite formation on the usual hanging left shoulder tab. Below his jump-wings the officer wears the ribbon of the second highest award for gallantry, the Ot Haoz, and those for the 1967 and 1973 wars. Prior to 1973 Israel had no gallantry medals as such, marking extreme gallantry by the solemn award of a parliamentary citation. The three grades now awarded are Ot Hamofet (plain blue ribbon), Ot Haoz (plain crimson), and the supreme gallantry award, the Ot Hagvura (plain yellow ribbon). On the left collar point the officer wears the Officer School graduation pin; on his right pocket flap the flaming sword of the Active Combat badge, and the Service in Occupied Territory badge; and on the left pocket flap the head-on silver tank badge marking a proficiency qualification in this branch.

A girl soldier of Nahal, off duty at the El Al settlement on the Golan Heights; she served as a radio operator in the 1973 War. (Author's collection)

G4: Sergeant parachute rigger, 202nd Airborne Bde., 1970s

The rank bars of this grade—Samal—are worn on the uniform illustrated at full length in Plate D1. The bonnet is in airborne maroon, and bears the Infantry badge pinned through scarlet. The brigade patch is worn in the conventional way; and note Rigger's badge in silver on left breast pocket above button—a motif combining wings, parachute, and two open hands.

G5: Recruit, Armoured Corps, 1970s

The graduation and swearing-in of a recruit are made the subject of considerable patriotic ceremony in Zahal. This lad is taken from a photo of a night-time torchlight parade on the summit of Mt. Masada, the Israelis' unofficial shrine to the memory of Jewish fighters who endured unto death. The 'Golani' Bde. hold ceremonies at the site of the ancient fort of Gamla on the Golan Heights. Typically, the recruit is handed his rifle —and sometimes a Bible—at the climax of the ceremony. The shoulder strap loop bearing a blue stripe is widely seen among recruits of all branches. The collar of the battledress blouse bears the same

miniature badges as Plate F2. The Corps beret bears a diamond-shaped badge specifically issued to recruits of all branches.

H1: Infantryman, Golan Heights, late 1970s

It gets extremely cold on the slopes of Mt. Hermon in winter, and this figure, taken from colour photos, is a reminder of the fact. He wears standard Zahal combat gear with the winter parka (note quilted lining showing in hood); the Israeli-made M-1 helmet with crossed straps, and the usual rubber edge-band applied; and woollen balaclava and gloves. Note that the weapon is the US M16.

H2: Paratroop officer, 1980

Photographed returning from a night mission over the frontier into the terrorist refuges of 'Fatah-land', this appears to be a junior officer. Note the crossed stripes on the helmet, which often coincide in photos with officer rank; and the 'blinker' light fixed in the helmet band at the back, for night station-keeping—an obvious accessory for a junior leader. He wears a heavy olive sweater and substantial gloves, carries the Galil assault rifle, and is displaying the front of the new Israeli web equipment.

H3: Infantryman, West Bank, 1981

Photographed on routine security patrol on the occupied West Bank of Jordan, this Zahal private soldier wears the current pattern of fatigues complete with a soft visored cap, and displays the rear of the new web equipment. Its very broad belt and straps distribute the weight well; it can be put on and off in one piece, like a jacket, while the lacing at four points allows infinite adjustment to individual size. The nine integral pouches, of five sizes, accommodate a great deal of equipment and ammunition; and note Velcro fastening of flaps, for speed and ease. This imaginative and battle-proven design is considered by some specialists to be the best in the world.

Further reading:

Men-at-Arms 128, *Arab Armies of the Middle East Wars 1948–73*, John Laffin; Osprey, London

Vanguard 19, *Armour of the Middle East Wars 1948–78*, Steven J. Zaloga; Osprey, London

Also:

The Hashemite Arab Army 1908–1979, Brig. S. A. El-Edroos; The Publishing Committee, Amman, Jordan

Above and Beyond, Yehuda Harel; Olive Books, Tel Aviv, Israel

The War of Atonement, Chaim Herzog; Weidenfeld & Nicolson, London

The Israeli Army, E. Luttwak & D. Horowitz; Allen Lane, London

No Victor, No Vanquished, E. O'Ballance; Barrie & Jenkins, London

The Anatomy of the Israeli Army, G. E. Rothenberg; Batsford, London

The Tanks of Tammuz, Shabtai Teveth, Weidenfeld & Nicolson

Various issues, *Born in Battle* series; Eshel-Dramit Ltd, Hod Hasharon, Israel

Details of the current Israeli-manufactured infantry combat equipment, made in nylon and developed from an American prototype. See Plates H2, H3. (Author's collection)

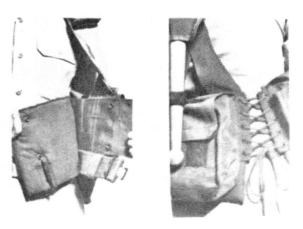

INDEX

Figures in **bold** refer to illustrations.